TOPGUN
MIRAMAR

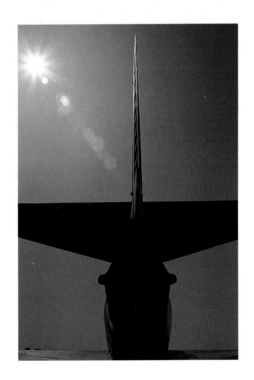

TOPGUN
MIRAMAR

DEAN GARNER
DONNA BRACKEEN

OSPREY
AEROSPACE

About the author

William Dean Anthony Garner, the son of an ex-Air Force F-4 driver, is a freelance writer and photographer, and has flown in various USAF jets including the F-4, F-15, F-16 and KC-135, as well as the US Navy's A-4, F-14, F-16 and C-2. He is currently doing postdoctoral research at Duke University.

Donna Michelle Brackeen, the daughter of a former aircraft designer and aerospace executive, was trained as a financial analyst in the aerospace industry. She is also a freelance writer and photographer.

Dedication

This volume is dedicated to Colonel William Darrell Garner, PhD (USAF, retired), Captain Donald Richard 'Blade' Armstrong Jnr, the memory of Richard Ennis Brackeen and the men and women of TOPGUN.

Published in 1992 by Osprey Publishing Limited
59 Grosvenor Street, London W1X 9DA

ISBN 1 855322463

Editor Tony Holmes
Photo captions Roy Braybrook
Design Paul Kime
Printed in Italy

HALF TITLE PAGE
An artistic composition from the flight-line of the US Navy Fighter Weapons School (NFWS), or TOPGUN establishment at NAS Miramar, California. Despite its age (the first of the Douglas A-4 Skyhawk series made its maiden flight on 22 June 1954), the A-4 still provides a good representation of opponents such as the MiG-17 and MiG-21 in air combat training

TITLE PAGE
View from the rear seat of an NFWS TA-4J, flown by Lt Bill 'Hack' McMasters, as it reaches a load factor of five-G over NAS North Island. The centreline structural canopy member underlines the fact that the hood must be jettisoned prior to ejection

RIGHT
Lt John 'Milt' Milton seated in the cockpit of his A-4E Skyhawk in front of the famed TOPGUN Hangar One at NAS Miramar. Design details include the essential array of rear-view mirrors on the aerodynamic, pressure-activated, leading-edge slats, which are readily moved by hand

Contents

Acknowledgements

This volume culminates almost two years of planning, designing and implementing a dream. A dream to fly with the finest, most lethal fighter pilots in the world, and to tell their story in words and pictures. However, our dream would not have been possible without the gracious support and co-operation of the US Navy and the Navy Fighter Weapons School – TOPGUN. We gratefully acknowledge the following individuals and organizations for their generous support:

Op-05 Pentagon
VADM Richard M Dunleavy; Lt Cdr Carl 'Brain' Braun; Lt Cdr George 'Elwood' Dom; and Mr John Maslin

TOPGUN
Cdr Bob 'Puke' McClane, Commander (2/92-present); Capt Jim 'Rookie' Robb, Commander (5/89-2/92); Lt Cdr Jerry 'Steamer' Beaman, Executive Officer; Maj Billy 'Stump' Miles, Operations Officer; Lt Cdr Jeff Taylor, Administrative Officer; Lt Bill 'Hack' McMasters, Media; Lt Jim 'Grits' Grimson, Safety; Lt Kirk 'Willie' Williams; Lt Mark 'Action' Jackson; Lt Dave 'Shooter' Vanderschoot, Training; Maj Tony 'Spike' Valentino; Lt John 'Milt' Milton, Maintenance; Capt Bob 'Jeckyll' Cotterell, Maintenance; Capt Pat 'Kato' Cooke, Training; Lt Tom 'Trim' Downing, Training; Lt Calvin 'Goose' Craig, Training; Lt Scott 'Sterno' Stearney, Operations; Lt Pete 'Skids' Matthews, Maintenance; Lt Mike 'Mikey' Jennings, Readiness; Lt Tom 'Clubber' Lang, Intelligence; Capt Mike 'Troll' Manuche, Safety; Capt Jim 'Gasm' Orr, Maintenance; Capt John 'Ajax' Neumann; Lt Sam 'Slammer' Richardson, Operations; Lt Doug 'Muddy' Waters; Capt Cletus 'Clete' Norris, Readiness; Maj Thom 'T-Mac' McCarthy; Lt John 'Rooster' Clagett, Maintenance; Ens Jon 'Lloyd' Nolan and Ens Rob 'Hooch' Turner; Mr Mel 'Spine Ripper' Horowitz, Intelligence; Ms Kathy Moore, Executive Secretary; Mr Greg Palmore, Media; YNl Terry Coons, Training; Seaman Alan 'Wrap' Reynolds, Administration; Mr Don Shetler, Manager, General Dynamics Aircraft Services facility; Mr Bill 'Midnight' Dollard, TACTS; Mr Dan Kuttner, Media; and the men and women of TOPGUN.

Navy Public Affairs/Media
Lts Beci Brenton, Lydia Zeller, Ken Ross and Tom Van Leunen; Lt(jg) Taylor Kiland; Senior Chief Pat Neal and Petty Officer Brian Ellis.

USS Ranger (CV-61)
Capt Dennis McGinn, Commanding Officer; Lt Rod Hill and Petty Officer Steve Fiebing, Public Affairs; Lt Rik Cutting; Chad Touchet and Jason Headrick; and the men of the *Ranger*

NAS Miramar
ATAN Jim Yows, NAS Miramar Police Department; the men and women of VF-211; Lts Dave Busse and Ray Butts, Ens Scott McQuillen, AMSl Jeff Pate, AMHl John Coffin and the men and women of VAW-110.

US Marine Corps
Capt Chris 'Cooker' Cooke and the men and women of VMFAT-101, MCAS El Toro

Special Contributors
Bill, Olga, John, Leil and Chaney Garner; Richard Brackeen, Karel, Debbie and Lori Brackeen and Susan McHan; Mr Jack Fisher; Hon Randy 'Duke' Cunningham and Mr Frank Purcell.

Foreword

by Honorable Randy 'Duke' Cunningham

BOTH THE Navy and the Marine Corps were rudely awakened by America's experience in Vietnam. Victory in battle requires a force to fight the war of the future. The US, in Vietnam, fought the battles of the past. Though Washington was convinced early on that technology would bring America victory, combat proved our technology insufficient. We entered the war ill-prepared, with equipment designed for an interceptor war, with fragile technology, vulnerable tactics, and insufficient training. My own McDonnell Douglas F-4 Phantom II, the premier fighter bomber of its generation, lacked a gun in front and a dogfight-trained pilot in the cockpit.

Such shortcomings brought about woefully low combat kill figures. Out of the thousands of Naval combat pilots assigned to the conflict, only two became aces, having downed five or more enemy aircraft — Lt(jg) Willie Driscoll, my RIO, and I.

We were among the first Naval aviators to reap the benefits of highly advanced fighter weapons training at TOPGUN, at NAS Miramar, California. We proved the truism that a pilot fights like he trains.

In the midst of the Vietnam war, the Navy had begun considering why American air combat against the Soviet-trained and equipped North Vietnamese was less than successful. In 1968, a need was recognized for improved weapons system reliability and training for crews headed for air combat.

Captain Frank Ault was commissioned to study the situation, analyze weaknesses, and recommend improvements. He suggested forming a graduate-level military school, chartered to train the best of the best – a nucleus of fighter aircrews, highly competent in aerial combat and the employment of weapons systems.

Beginning as an offshoot of the Pacific Fleet F-4 replacement training squadron, TOPGUN convened its first class in March 1969, and was formally commissioned in July 1972. No one envisioned at that time that the world's finest school of air-to-air combat had been born.

TOPGUN was in its early days when I entered the fleet in 1969. Between my first and second combat cruises to Vietnam, we flew against TOPGUN instructors and honed our skills. Everyone trained harder and improved their tactics. The fact that I downed five enemy MiGs on my second combat cruise is testi-

CUNNINGHAM/DRISCOLL
10 MAY 72
VF-96

CUNNINGHAM/DRISCOLL
10 MAY 72
VF-96

CONNELLY/BLONSKI
10 MAY 72
VF-96

CUNNINGHAM/DRISCOLL
10 MAY 72
VF-96

CANNON/MORRIS
10 MAY 72
VF-51

CONNELLY/BLONSKI
10 MAY 72
VF-96

CUNNINGHAM/DRISCOLL
10 MAY 72
VF-96

LEFT

TOPGUN's inspirational graduate Randy 'Duke' Cunningham (then a US Navy lieutenant and currently a US congressman) reflects on 10 May 1972, when he and his RIO, Lt (jg) William 'Irish' Driscoll, jointly destroyed three North Vietnamese Air Force MiG-17s. They were flying an F-4J from the USS Constellation (CV-64) as part of VF-96 'Fighting Falcons', and had already delivered Rockeye cluster bombs against a storage building when the engagements occurred. This day brought their scores to five enemy aircraft, and their last engagement terminated Col Tomb, North Vietnam's ranking ace, who was credited with at least 13 victories against US aircraft

mony to the effects advanced TOPGUN training had on my own capabilities. Following the war, I returned to TOPGUN as an instructor. The School was formally commissioned, and word of its high quality spread. Having gone months in Vietnam without a single MiG kill in combat, the Navy found that 60 per cent of its combat kills were scored by TOPGUN graduates. That was a number the admirals in Washington understood.

Today, TOPGUN celebrates its 25th year. What started as a resolution, a gleam in the eye of Captain Ault and a few frustrated Navy combat pilots, has become the home of the world's finest air-to-air combat training. Its success inspired the Air Force to create Red Flag. And from its beginning at NAS Miramar, TOPGUN has expanded to include five smaller weapons schools at master jet bases across the country, plus an entire 150-aircraft adversary system challenging the world's best fighter pilots.

None of this existed when I started flying. We are only left to imagine what our successes would have been had we started TOPGUN-style air combat training from the beginning.

But Vietnam, and even the Cold War, are over. This, the best news in two generations, is not without its difficulties. While the Pentagon and Congress struggle with restructuring the post-Cold War national defence – how much to cut, when, where, and so on – there can be no higher priority than the training and equipping of our combat aviators, ground troops and sailors. Such training saves lives, both in the air and among the troops on the ground and sailors at sea.

As a member of Congress myself, I have returned to TOPGUN many times to get briefings on the current threat and developments in tactics. Each time, the instructors are better than the last. Each time their scope expands. Each time their recommendations are incredibly well researched and polished.

The services of TOPGUN are requested by every major Western military power, and their impact is felt by the rest. And, as military planners develop and produce strike fighter aircraft for the 21st century, TOPGUN expertise will shape the way they are used.

All along, TOPGUN has been about the future, preparing America's elite Naval combat aviators for the battles we hope will never come. I'm honoured to have played a small part of it.

I hope you will enjoy Dean Garner's outstanding collection of TOPGUN anecdotes and photographs. Perhaps you will find you, too, have the 'right stuff' for TOPGUN. Check six!

Introduction

by Commander Robert L 'Puke' McClane, Commanding Officer

THE NAVY flies the finest, most lethal aircraft in the world. But, perhaps more important, we train. We train to the most likely threat. We train to the most formidable enemy. That's where we really make our money, finding ways to better use the hardware at our disposal. And obviously that's where TOPGUN comes into the picture.

The Navy Fighter Weapons School is probably the most publicized squadron in Naval history. But with all that has been written and recorded about the school, Dean Garner's book brings an important, new perspective to an organization often characterized with swaggering young fighter pilots wearing G-suits and Darth Vader-like helmets.

As Dean began this project, he immersed himself wholly in day-to-day operations. Curiously, he is one of the few freelance photographers to sample the viewpoint of the men and women behind the scenes in the administrative and maintenance departments. These unheralded people perform a vital function and deserve much of the credit for the School's success. He intuitively sensed this fact.

Briefing, flying, and living with the men and women at TOPGUN is not an easy task. The School is a smorgasbord of action, from traditional air combat training missions against Navy and Marine Corps students, to developing better tactics against emerging threats. Dean became personally involved with our mission, sharing our camaraderie, job satisfaction and frustrations. His is a unique perspective, one that characterizes the School as an organization of professionals dedicated to excellence. I believe you will find Dean's volume a very accurate portrayal of the real TOPGUN.

One of the most asked questions we receive is 'What's air combat really like?' Typically, it's gut wrenching, confusing and physically demanding. A pilot finds himself drawing on all his experience, intuition, and cleverness in a fight to the death . . . a duel of men and machines. Imagine the stress of being subjected to eight times your body weight. But you must still think a couple of moves ahead, as in chess. Your fingers must shift deftly from switch to switch in the cockpit, selecting different radar modes, bringing up the correct missile or the 20 mm gun, all the while 'checking six', keeping track of your wingman, and continually re-analyzing the situation. Needless to say, the aircrews are tasked to their limits, both mentally and physically.

But there's more. You need a gameplan. Just as pro football offensive co-ordinators tailor their plans from week to week, based on the next defence, we also analyze our opponent and fly our fighters to leverage our good points against his limitations. For example, you will hear fighter pilots talk for hours about performance. We typically use two parameters to compare aircraft performance: agility and speed. Agility is the ability of an aircraft to rapidly change direction. Why is that important? Today's fighter must point its nose at the opponent to employ guns or missiles effectively. The nose of the fighter is the business end of the aeroplane. The first aircraft to point at the other is often the winner, everything else being equal.

We used to have a saying, 'Speed is life'. There is a lot truth in that statement. A fast aeroplane has more options available than a slower fighter. The quicker aeroplane may leave the fight if things aren't going well, getting outside missile range before the more agile aircraft can turn and shoot. In effect, running away to fight another day. Conversely, the faster aircraft may be able to 'track down' a slower, escaping fighter.

More and more, we hear about stealthiness, the ability to mask our presence and deny reaction time to the enemy. Most of today's fighter crews would say that speed and agility are at least as important as stealthiness. Stealthiness will complement traditional performance measures, not replace them!

What do the Navy and Marine Corps get out of TOPGUN? We train aircrews to be winners. And what makes a winner? Preparation, good equipment, proficiency and, more than anything else, mental attitude. The mental toughness that makes a winner spells the difference between success and failure in air combat. And, in our business, that translates to life and death.

We graduate 60 aircrews (F-14 and F/A-18) a year, who are tasked with spreading the 'tactical gospel' to the fleet. These young officers are brought up to speed on the latest tactical doctrine, while receiving one of the most intensive flying syllabi in the world. But that's just the beginning. From TOPGUN, they return to their respective squadrons to nurture those aircrews and stimulate air-to-air training. And what will you find in those operational fighter squadrons? Patriotic, well-trained men who fix and fly the best aircraft available. . .take pride in their work and are confident in their ability to bring the fight to the enemy . . . to park off his shore and 'project power'.

And what is 'power projection'? That means establishing air superiority (shooting down his MiGs), blasting his surface-to-air missile system apart and destroying targets with air-to-ground weapons. No one else in the world can do that as quickly and effectively as a deployed Carrier Battle Group! It's an awesome capability that hinges on training – training that TOPGUN helps provide.

PREVIOUS PAGE
Another day, another dollar. NFWS instructor Marine Corps Capt Bob 'Jeckyll' Coterell banks his F-16N to port and heads back to NAS Miramar. The General Electric F110-powered F-16N is reckoned to give a reasonable representation of modern fourth generation fighters such as the MiG-29 Fulcrum and the Su-27 Flanker

Chapter one
TOPGUN
Instructors

'**T**HE HOLLYWOOD image of a fighter pilot is in stark contrast to the reality of our profession. We are trained assassins. We draw our strength from the warriors of the past. Men who have made the ultimate sacrifice to ensure the freedom of others. Our job at TOPGUN is to ensure that the US Navy and Marine Corps fighter pilots are the most highly trained and lethal fighter pilots in the world. We must always remember that, no matter how technologically advanced we may become, it all comes down to the man in the machine!' – Lieutenant Tom 'Trim' Downing, Instructor

This fiercely competitive spirit is shared by all pilots and radar intercept officers (RIOs). TOPGUN's fighting spirit draws energy primarily from its instructors, the leaders of the school. All of the instructors are hand picked from Navy and Marine Corps fleet squadrons. Also, there is usually one US Air Force instructor, who has successfully completed the USAF's Fighter Weapons School course at Miramar.

'There has always been a tradition of co-operation and mutual respect between the Air Force Fighter Weapons School and the Navy Fighter Weapons School. Everyone asks me how the two compare, and I have to say it's apples and oranges. The goal in the end is the same; produce a tactical expert who can teach the other bubbas to be the best tacticians possible. No matter what kind of uniform he wears, a fighter pilot is a fighter pilot. Although I miss the operational F-15 world, it's quite a ride flying A-4s and F-16s!'

Regardless of where they have come from, TOPGUN instructors all share the inexorable will to be the best in their respective field, and to pass on to their eager students their unique skills.

The average TOPGUN instructor is about 32 years old, and has about seven years of experience flying in high performance jets. He has a distinctive edge of

OVERLEAF

The US Navy's Lt Scott 'Sterno' Stearny and USAF exchange pilot Capt Cletus 'Clete' Norris, respectively mounted in an F-16N and A-4F, are pictured en route to mixing it with Navy F/A-18 Hornets. The '45' code of the F-16N indicates that it is BuNo 163272, while A-4F '54' is clearly BuNo 154172

*A quintet of TOPGUN instructors: from left to right, USMC Maj Billy 'Stump' Miles, Navy
Lt Mark 'Action' Jackson, USMC Maj Tony 'Spike' Valentino, Navy Lt Bill 'Hack'
McMasters and Navy Lt Jim 'Grits' Grimson, pictured after 'Spike's' last TOPGUN flight*

aggressiveness, controlled and honed by dedication, perseverance, and strict discipline. He is quite cocky and dominant. He's a thrill seeker, living many aspects
of his life on the edge. He's also a weight lifter, arising at five am to pump hundreds of pounds of iron in the TOPGUN weight room. He's also a mechanic, a
father, a gardener, a car racer, a sailor.

Intellectually, our average TOPGUN instructor has a high IQ, although he is
too modest to admit it. Our instructor assimilates masses of data in a short period
of time. He regurgitates only the pertinent aspects of his work to other instructors and students, avoiding the minutiae.

Although seemingly selfish, the instructor is a team player, fighting not only
for himself in mock battles, but also for his wingman, his flight lead, his flight
element. What's good for the team is good for him.

The TOPGUN philosophy fosters a group effort. Yet, it allows one's individual personality to emerge and add his unique flavour to the group. This
freedom allows individual psychological and social growth within the unit.
Moreover, it helps contribute to the overall TOPGUN atmosphere.

'Dedication is the key word here at TOPGUN. The instructors are not that
much different from most pilots in the Navy and Marine Corps. It's just that the
opportunities exist here to practice ACM on a fairly regular basis and, most
importantly, recall, analyze and teach the fights extensively. And that requires
dedication, which is usually brought with the instructor when he walks through
the door on his first day. Or, it is impressed on him through peer pressure.

USMC Capt Jim 'Gasm' Orr, photographed immediately prior to a brief. An instructor's assignment at NFWS normally represents a three-year posting

Either way, to survive and do well at TOPGUN requires dedication.' – Lieutenant Calvin 'Goose' Craig, Instructor

From individual personalities sprout the badge of this modern-day warrior – the call sign. Many instructors' call signs were taken from their own names. Capt Cletus 'Clete' Norris, an F-15 driver in his previous life with the USAF, prizes his Oklahoma-born name. The stocky 'Clete' has a not-so-rough side, too, often allowing some of it to slip out. Although the moniker is tough, the man is genuinely humane. While all TOPGUN instructors share 'Clete's' soft side, even though they may not always reveal it, their call signs would suggest otherwise. Lt Bill 'Hack' McMasters, the ham of the bunch, is a stocky, six-foot-two, two hundred twenty pounds of Mr Nice Guy. The name 'Hack' suggests a starring role in Halloween VI, and he portrays just that while flying ACM . But when the show's over, he heads off to the 'Hack Hacienda', some 28 miles into the hills of rural southern California, where he's installing PVC piping to water his yard and garden, or contemplating which species of shrub to plant in the front yard. And when the work is done, he sits in front of a roaring fire, drinking beer from a frozen TOPGUN mug, and unwinds to a re-run of 'The Simpsons'.

Other pilots' call signs are derived from amusing associations, like Lt Dave 'Flea' Markert, a RIO. 'Flea's' crack sense of humour and gift of the gab leave you feeling like you're in the company of a gregarious cousin, polishing off a six-pack of Budweiser by the pond.

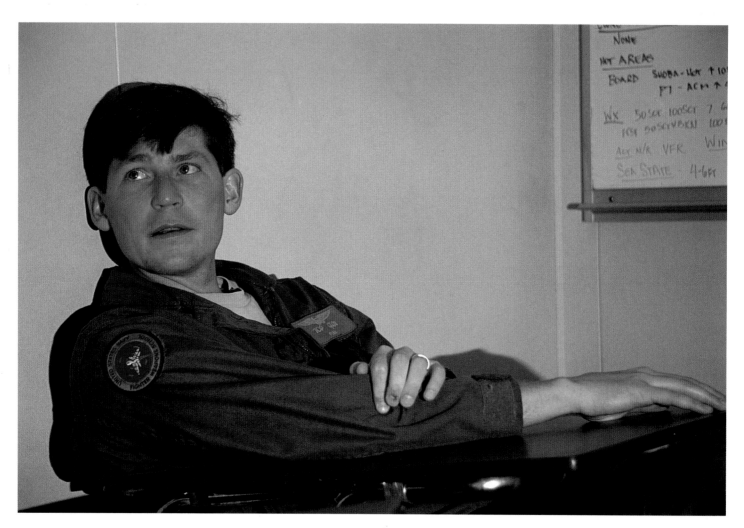

ABOVE LEFT
Navy Lt Dave 'Flea' Markert, pictured relaxing before a brief. This instructor serves as a RIO on the F-14

LEFT
USAF Capt Cletus 'Clete' Norris, an Oklahoma-born former F-15 pilot, studies A-4 tactics before a brief

ABOVE
Navy Lt John 'Rooster' Clagett, Capt Cletus 'Clete' Norris and Navy Lt Sam 'Slammer' Richardson discuss the day's flight schedules in the TOPGUN ready-room

If there was ever an anachronism at TOPGUN, it's Lt Jim 'Grits' Grimson. 'Hack' aptly calls 'Grits' the 'Boy Pilot'. With very young, handsome, boyish looks and inexorable charm, 'Grits' is seemingly right out of the first row of a tenth-grade literature class.

Some call signs, however, are from memorable occasions – near-death events, as some recall. TOPGUN's skipper, Cdr Bob 'Puke' McClane, is a shining example, although he might like to forget those infamous 24 hours many years ago. During his initial flight training in the F-8 Crusader, 'Puke' and the guys worked hard and played harder. One morning, after a long niqht of imbibing no-name spirits, McClane went on a vomiting binge. 'I puked all night, puked when I woke up, and puked before, during and after the brief. The only I time I felt good was when I was flying. After then, I dry-heaved all day.' The squadron got together and voted on what to nickname the illustrious Bob McClane. Let there be 'Puke'.

ABOVE

USMC Capt Mike 'Troll' Manuche talks with an incoming F-14 Tomcat pilot, as he lands after a mission

RIGHT

Capt Cletus 'Clete' Norris carries out a visual preflight inspection of his A-4 Skyhawk. The aircraft's camouflage scheme is only one of several used by the NFWS

Maj Billy 'Stump' Miles fits the part, too. At five-foot eight or so, he's built like a Rottweiler, weighing in at about 190 lbs. As with the other wild-eyed fighter pilots, 'Stump's' gregarious personality overshadows his rocky features. And as TOPGUN's Operations Officer, he's the guy who keeps the fighters fighting, the coach.

Will the real 'Action' Jackson please stand up? No, he's not Carl Weathers. He has prominent facial features, including an infectious grin. The sandy-voiced Tomcat driver lives by his name at altitude, ringing the death knell and wreaking mass destruction.

Colourful personalities aside, the instructors at the school are top notch, not only as aviators but as managers and teachers. They go to TOPGUN to hone their skills in many different areas, making them highly competitive executives.
'I have always been impressed with the professionalism displayed by the TOPGUN staff and their absolute expertise in fighter tactics. The flying during the five-week class was against some of the world's best, and I was never disappointed with their presentation of the various threat scenarios.

'The debriefs were thorough and extremely informative, always leaving the student with a positive attitude, regardless of the outcome. The lectures were by far the most impressive aspect of the course. The instructors are the Navy/Marine experts on all aspects of fighter tactics and were very approachable if a question came to mind' – Marine Corps Capt Chris 'Cooker' Cooke VMFAT-101, F/A-18 Air-to-Air Training Phase Head, TOPGUN Class 6-86

Flying is only a small, albeit a very important part of the job as a TOPGUN instructor. Each instructor is given a topic to study, one in which he will become an expert, regardless of whether he is familiar with the background material. And he studies, researches, outlines, and writes, until he is prepared to

LEFT
Half hidden by a visor that protects against the sun's rays and incoming birds, Navy Lt John 'Milt' Milton prepares for take-off in another officer's A-4. This photograph emphasizes the small size of the Skyhawk cockpit, compared to those of more modern aircraft such as the F-14 and F-15

ABOVE
One for the family album: Navy Lt Bill 'Hack' McMasters poses in front of his NFWS F-16N at sunset, modelling a March 1992 collection of fighter pilot apparel in the process

defend his thesis at a 'murder board'. The 'murder board' is an intensive four-hour-plus defence of an instructor's lecture plan. This is the briefing he'll be pontificating to students. He presents his work in front of other instructors, including the commanding officer, executive officer, and operations officer, the top three men at TOPGUN. Interestingly, the upper-level officers carry no more weight in a 'murder board' than do the younger instructors. Regardless, the instructors grill him, coach him, and forge him into an efficient professor of, for example, infrared missiles or one-v-one aerial combat, or surface-to-air missiles, or threat aircraft. Like 24-carat gold, highly malleable and priceless, the instructor now is prepared to pass onto his students much-prized knowledge, gleaned from decades of Cold War and strained peace, and actual aerial combat.

'TOPGUN, due primarily to the movie, has a worldwide approval. As a TOPGUN instructor, my exposure to fighter training worldwide has been great. The worldwide emphasis and appeal was driven home when I was training with some European units. One day, we were strolling through a farmers' market in Belgium, and we came across a young man wearing a TOPGUN jacket. We

LEFT

Although General Dynamics may have provided the ground crew member, the aircraft is a Grumman F-14 Tomcat, one of several operated by the NFWS to provide back-up for students' aircraft and for instructor proficiency checks. In this instance the RIO, Lt Doug 'Muddy' Waters, is performing preflight checks in the rear cockpit of 'Red 32'

ABOVE

USMC Capt Pat 'Kato' Cooke bakes in the cockpit of his F-16N as he waits in the hold-short area for an F-14 to land and clear the runway. This photograph illustrates both of the camouflage schemes that have been applied to the F-16N, that in the foreground appearing only on '42' (BuNo 163269)

explained to him that we were from TOPGUN, via business cards, etc, and we were instantly his lifelong friends. He could not do enough for us! I'm sure he had seen his fair share of US military, but he took a shining to us!' – Lieutenant Dave 'Flea' Markert, Instructor

Is there life after TOPGUN? After flying at least once every week-day for three years with the hottest fighter pilots in the world where does one go? Seemingly, other jobs pale in comparison. But the fun is just beginning. Now it's time to move up the corporate ladder, implementing those skills in management, leadership, and teaching.

Many instructors graduate to fleet roles as an operations or executive officer. Some even progress to commanding a fleet squadron. Further on in their careers, some command aircraft carriers. The shrewd often go into high-level

LEFT
Meanwhile, up at the sharp end, the Tomcat's pilot, Lt Jim 'Grits' Grimson, carries out his own cockpit checks and prepares to haul the F-14 off Miramar's concrete

ABOVE
'Kato' joins up with the F-14 camera ship in the second F-16N off the line. A total of 26 F-16Ns were built for the US Navy, with serials in the range 163268-281 and 163566-577. The four two-seat TF-16Ns are serialled 163278-281. Aside from those at NFWS, there are F-16Ns at VF-43 'Challengers' at NAS Oceana, Virginia, VF-45 'Blackbirds' at NAS Key West, Florida, and VF-126 'Bandits' at Miramar. In a recent nose-count there were seven each at the NFWS and VF-45 NFWS, and six with each of the other units. TOPGUN has two two-seaters and VF-43 and -45 one apiece

executive positions in the Pentagon, designing and implementing tactical and strategic plans to ensure that Naval Aviation remains at the top.

Ultimately though, the TOPGUN warriors must retire, some leaving the service to enter politics, academics, and corporate business.

'Intelligence alone will not make a person a TOPGUN instructor. Aggressiveness, athletics, and a natural desire for competition and the will to win are paramount to a successful fighter pilot. The pilots who also possess a shrewd intellect are the ones who wind up at TOPGUN.' – Lt Bill 'Hack' McMasters, Instructor

Chapter two
TOPGUN Students

THE HEART and soul of this place is derived from the students that come here. They not only provide us with our reason for existence, but they also inject us with the energy needed to keep our standards up to their challenges'. – Marine Corps Capt Bob 'Jeckyll' Cotterell, Instructor

As with the instructors, TOPGUN draws its students from the US Navy and Marine Corps fighter squadrons. Students chosen to attend the Power Projection course are the best potential instructor pilots the fleet can offer. Each squadron has one slot (one pilot, or one pilot and one RIO), every 12 to 18 months. Therefore, only the most talented pilots and RIOs with instructor potential are awarded the slot. Each student has, on average, more than 500 hours in their respective aircraft, plus at least one overseas carrier deployment. Beyond the quantitative criteria, it takes a special knack for leading, managing and teaching.

Students have diverse college backgrounds, from mechanical engineering to political science. One need not be a rocket scientist to fly high-performance aircraft. It takes a thinker who can execute a well thought out plan. A good 'stick' with excellent hand-eye co-ordination isn't enough. Brain power is essential. Topping off the apparently endless list of qualifying criteria is the ability to interact well with peers, and both senior and junior personnel.

After selection to attend TOPGUN, students fly their home squadron's aircraft to Miramar, where they are pitted against TOPGUN instructors flying the A-4 Skyhawk, F-16 Viper, and F-14 Tomcat. The Skyhawk effectively simulates the older second and third generation threat aircraft, like the MiG-17 and MiG-21. The 'Viper' mimics the latest, fourth-generation threats like the Mirage 2000, MiG-29, and Su-27. The Tomcat is used primarily for instructor proficiency and to augment student aircraft, rather than simulate MiGs.

The course itself is an intensive six weeks long. Each class consists of about eight to sixteen students, and about eight fighter aircraft – F-14s and F/A-18s. The School emphasizes a 'building-block' approach to teaching. It starts out relatively simply, but then newer, more difficult scenarios are progressively added. The first week is an intense academics phase in which students meet with the instructors, get a course syllabus, and start 60 hours of fleet-renowned tactical classroom instruction. Then, during the second week, it's off to the flightline to

stuff themselves into their fighting machines and each fly one-v-one sorties against a TOPGUN instructor. Students' performances are evaluated by the instructors, and then critiqued in extensive debriefings lasting several hours. A typical day lasts 12 hours. After that, it's time to let the newly acquired data ferment, and passively allow their subconcious minds to further process the volatile end-product.

Following a blazing first two weeks, students next practice section tactics-two aircraft working together to design and implement a mission versus an unknown number of threat aircraft. 'Two versus X,' they call it. Still building on the lessons learned in weeks one, two and three, students enter the fourth week studying division tactics, or four aircraft; working together.

Weeks five and six teach further aspects of division tactics, culminating in week six's deployment to a nearby naval air station or Air Force base. The class executes four, detailed, highly involved strikes against unknown aircraft, using ground controllers and other mission-support personnel to effect their plan.

After graduating from the Power Projection course, students return to the fleet, where they become squadron training officers. Their task now is to teach squadron members the latest in aerial weapons and tactics, and advise the squadron command on matters pertinent to the tactical mission.

With hard work, perseverance, outstanding performance in the course, and strong recommendations, a student can be selected to become one of the chosen few – a TOPGUN instructor – spending three years at TOPGUN, flying up to 12 times a week, concentrating on practicing, and teaching and flying simulated air combat.

PREVIOUS PAGE
Instructor Lt John 'Milt' Milton walks out to his Skyhawk, which is painted in desert camouflage. The code '50' identifies this as an A-4F, BuNo 155000. The automatic leading-edge slats and the vortex generators are indicative of the problems Douglas had in developing a useful buffet lift coefficient from this cropped delta wing. The planform was adopted to combine light weight and large area with a short span, thus avoiding the need for a wing-fold, but it has a tendency tot tip-stall

LEFT
Wide-angle self-portrait of the author in the rear seat of a TOPGUN TA-4J, with Lts Scott 'Sterno' Stearney and Pete 'Skids' Matthews flying echelon starboard in their TF-16N, with everything down and airbrakes out

ABOVE

Two of TOPGUN's instructors (Lts Waters and Milton) chat with visiting 'MiG killer' Lt Nick 'Mongo' Mongillo in the main hallway of the NFWS. 'Mongo' scored the fourth kill of the Gulf War while flying his F/A-18C (BuNo 163502) with VFA-81 'Sunliners' as part of CVW-17 (code AA), operating from the USS Saratoga (CV-60). A section of four Hornets were en route to attack a ground target when they were intercepted by two Chinese-built MiG-21s (F-7As) of the Iraqi Air Force. Both of these aircraft were shot down by the Hornets using AIM-9 Sidewinders

RIGHT

A mixed box of TOPGUN A-4s and F-16Ns in a climbing turn over the California coastline. By coincidence, both designs adopted modified delta wings; the A-4 for compactness and the F-16 for low wave drag, although both manufacturers were attracted by the light weight associated with a sharp taper

OVERLEAF

Twilight time: Lt Bill 'Hack' McMasters turns on the navigation lights of his F-16N. The name 'Viper', evidently adopted informally by Navy personnel for this General Dynamics aircraft, was the title originally favoured by the manufacturer. However, the USAF did not agree, and adopted the name 'Fighting Falcon', which is seldom used in practice

Rear quarter view from the TA-4J of two contrasting F-16Ns. The aircraft in the foreground was in fact the first F-16N built (BuNo 163268, coded '02'), and on this mission was flown by Capt 'Clete' Norris

ABOVE
Two NFWS 'Vipers' climb through a California sunset. The lead F-16N is flown by Lt Bill 'Hack' McMasters, while the TF-16N in trail houses USMC Maj Bill 'Stump' Miles and Lt Calvin 'Goose' Craig

RIGHT
Its desert camouflage contrasting with the blue of the Pacific, this F-16N banks to port, emphasizing its cropped delta wing planform. The purpose of the two sensors mounted on the intake duct is not clear, but they may be IR search and track devices

LEFT

The standard US Navy grey camouflage of this TOPGUN F-14A provides little contrast with either the cloud or the snow-capped mountains over which it is flying. Note the NFWS insignia on the vertical tail

ABOVE

The Tomcat, coded '33' and flown by Lt Tom 'Trim' Downing and Lt Calvin 'Goose' Craig, is joined in this shot by Lt Bill 'Hack' McMasters, flying F-16N '42' (BuNo 163269)

OVERLEAF

Probably the finest patrol-interceptor ever developed, the F-14 has for most of its life lacked the thrust that it was originally intended to receive, and this has limited its usefulness in the dogfight role. On the other hand its Hughes AWG-9 (the first pulse-Doppler radar to be fitted to a production fighter) and its two-man crew give it an advantage over most aircraft in terms of detection range and long-range target identification. Given suitable rules of engagement, the Tomcat can blow the enemy away before he has the chance to fire his own missiles

Chapter three
The Air-to-Air Tactical Brief

BEFORE THE fun begins, the fighter pilots must first plan their sortie. Planning and presenting an effective, well-conceived and concise air-to-air tactical brief requires hours of preparation. Even after a few years of experience, it's still tough to effectively convey all pertinent points about a mission. Normally, younger pilots learn necessary skills from older, experienced crews, – especially Training Officers – those who've graduated from TOPGUN. But even after a tour at TOPGUN, a fighter pilot must continually polish his briefing skills.

Early morning launches at TOPGUN mean waking up at five am, and hustling off to the squadron before six. A cup of coffee keeps the pilot company as he sketches out in brightly coloured pens the general plan of the hop: type of mission; number and type of aircraft; the area in which they will set-up and fight; time of launch; time of engagements; and emergency procedures, both on the ground and in the air. Next, the pilot sketches the basic plan of the fight. How the 'good' guys and 'bad' guys will be situated just before the engagement begins.

After all the salient data is illustrated on the board, it's time to call in the other men who will be involved in the morning's match. One or two, perhaps more, pilots will join him in the briefing room for between 30 to 60 minutes of detailed planning. The instructor leads the other pilots through all standard operating procedures, then concentrates on the tactical plan.

The rules of engagement are relatively simple: don't hit anyone. Too often during training exercises, inexperienced, or just plain careless, pilots have dropped their guard just long enough to get themselves killed, and drag down another innocent pilot, too. Normally, TOPGUN pilots recognize and highly respect the standard 500 hundred foot bubble around each aircraft. This means, don't get within 500 hundred feet of the other aircraft. Even with the best of planning, shit happens. All pilots know that. They also recognize that it's usually pilot error that gets someone killed. No one will talk about that sensitive topic, though. Let the chaplain or medical examiner or flight safety board member explain it.

Set-ups are very routine. Opposing aircraft, if they know their starting positions, will begin flying either head-on or in the same direction, only to

manoeuvre so as to break hard into their opponent. The head-on engagements typically start at about two miles, resulting either in a punch in the face or a high-aspect visual pass. The former is more desirable, since a guy can paint the bandit on radar, get either a radar or infrared signature of the aircraft, and then shoot him in the face with a simulated radar-guided AIM-7 Sparrow (fox-one), or heat-seeking AIM-9 Sidewinder missile (fox-two). Today's Navy pilots also have the option of a fox-three, using the state-of-the-art Phoenix missile or AMRAAM (Advanced Medium Range Air-to-Air Missile), both of which can track its own target without the aid of the mother aircraft's radar. Fire and forget. The ultimate way to kill your opponent; find him first without him seeing you, gun him into the ground, then cruise back to the ranch for a cold one.

Other useful aids talked about in the brief include using the TACTS (Tactical Air Combat Training System) controllers to guide and co-ordinate an air combat engagement. A TACTS controller is also very helpful in 'kill removal'-removing via preplanned communications the aircraft shot down during the simulated dogfight. Effective 'kill removal' alleviates potential mid-air collisions, and allows the guys who are still alive to continue to execute their tactics.

In addition to discussing offensive tactics using missiles or guns, the instructor adds defensive tactics. Just in case the bandit has his pipper on your tail feathers, it's good to know that you've got magnesium flares, which burn hot enough to attract a heat-seeking missile – a personalized bullet headed up your glowing tail pipes. Chaff, another expendable decoy, consists of long strips of aluminium designed to clutter a radar signal. Chaff serves as a countermeasure to radar-guided missiles. There's also ECM (Electronic Counter Measures), which electronically jam or clutter enemy radar signals.

Even with this high-tech software and space-age hardware, things sometimes go awry, so the instructor talks about emergency procedures. Punching out of an uncontrollable aircraft at 400 knots into a sub-zero abyss. Sometimes the worst does happen. And so these possibilities are discussed thoroughly, and their potential solutions emphasized. Even on the ground, waiting to taxy to the runway, life can take a wrong turn. An engine may explode, the cockpit electronics may overheat and catch on fire, the oxygen tank may rupture and explode. Ground egress, although not emphasized heavily in the brief, is always on the mind of a pilot. Somewhere, back in his subconscious (the seat of male intuition), an inner voice is running through a check list of emergency procedures. Conscientious pilots know this. They respect that voice.

ABOVE
Lt John 'Milt' Milton prepares to give his lecture

RIGHT
'Milt' reviews the latest NFWS student flight statistics

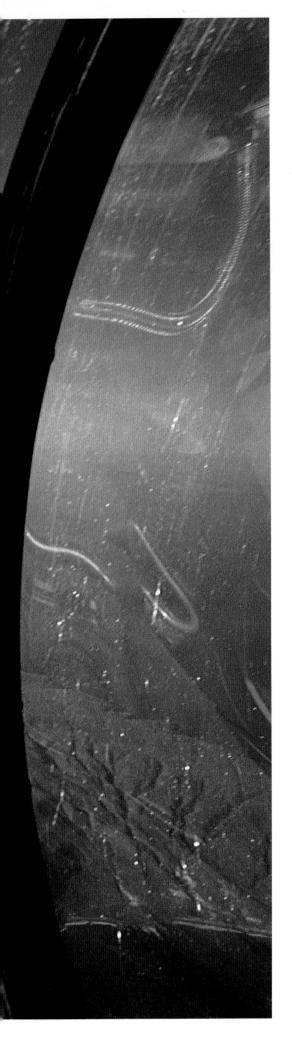

Chapter four
The Air-to-Air Mission

'THE BEST to way to have fun flying is to fight and win!' – Lieutenant Mark 'Action' Jackson, Instructor

The contents of the brief firmly on his mind, Lt Tom 'Trim' Downing scans over his G suit, looking for any obvious wear and tear. 'Looks good', he thinks, and zips up the waist and legs of the balloon-filled corsette that will add an extra G of tolerance during a high-G manoeuvre. Today, there will be many. The survival vest and parachute harness check out, too. Like a young Wall Street broker casually slipping into an Armani jacket, 'Trim' dons the vest and harness. The weight is noticeable, the fit slightly uncomfortable. Soon, any feelings of discomfort will dissipate when he steps into his executive office on the flightline – the F-14.

Before walking to his jet, 'Trim' puts leg-restraining straps on both lower legs. They will attach to a metal clip and thick nylon cord in the cockpit. If 'Trim' and his RIO ever had to bail out, the restrainer cord would pull in their legs during the ejection. At a slow speed ejection, it may be overkill. However, during a high-speed ejection, when a body is shooting into a 400 knot head wind, even the strongest arms and legs will be unceremoniously ripped from the torso, resulting in death by massive loss of blood.

This gruesome scene, although taught in flight training, does not enter 'Trim's' consciousness. He's devoting all brain power to the successful completion of his mission. Optimism. Think only positive thoughts. Leave the negatives to the losers.

'Trim' steps out to his jet, where Lt Mike 'Mikey' Jennings, the RIO, is looking over the Tomcat for obvious cracks and leaks. 'Trim' joins in and, soon after, the two complete the ground preflight checks. They both climb aboard their ride, and initiate more checks. 'Trim', the driver, co-ordinates many of his checks with the plane captain. They ensure that the movable surfaces of the wings and stabilators and twin tails are operating the way the book says. If not, the mission is over. An aborted flight is worse than your parents forgetting your 18th birthday.

Today, though, everything is a go, and running according to plan. While 'Trim' and the plane captain make final checks on the little things that make the big bird fly, 'Mikey' is flipping countless switches. He turns on the UHF radio, switches the TACAN (tactical aid for navigation) to '33' – NAS Miramar. He then positions the ejection select lever to 'MCO', which will allow either man to eject the duo upon pulling his ejection handle. He aligns the inertial navigation system, so the jet has a reference point from which to navigate. He punches in Miramar's co-ordinates of latitude and longitude, and waits for the radar screen to come alive. 'Mikey' then switches to 'Tactical Mode' on the radar panel, and prepares his visual displays for the upcoming dogfight. If they are going to beat the other guy – a TOPGUN F-16 'Viper', masquerading as a Soviet MiG-29 – before being seen, either visually or electronically, 'Mikey's' fire-control radar may be the key. 'Mikey' can direct the radar beam to cover a large volume of air space. The electromagnetic waves bounce off a target and return to 'Mikey's' machine, where they are processed and interpreted.

'Mikey' then activates many other computers on the CAP (computer address panel), and watches all the panel lights come to full brightness. The RIO cockpit is aglow with hundreds of red, green, yellow, white and blue lights, all signalling that 'Mikey's' office is open for business. Out of habit, 'Mikey' then double-checks his hardware and software. All is well. No breaks. No cracks. No fluid leaks. No unusual noises. No smoke. No fires.

'Trim' pulls out of the TOPGUN parking lot and taxies to the Hold Short area. More checks and double checks and triple checks. Redundancy means safety. Safety means life. Many hours of reading, studying, writing, donning, stepping, pushing, punching, switching, turning-and just waiting are about to culminate. The F-14 gets a shove-off signal from the young sailor and the folks in the air traffic control tower, and rolls out onto the runway. Like two little boys, dying to blow out the candles and dig into their jointly shared chocolate birthday cake, while being held back by their mothers, 'Trim' and 'Mikey' sit hungrily, mentally eyeing their upcoming feast.

'We're outta here', says a relieved 'Trim' on the intercom. The Tomcat glides down the road more than a mile, then leaps off the ground like its namesake, looking for trouble.

'TOPGUN 33, maintain 2000 feet, heading two-nine-zero. . .Have a good day', calls Miramar tower.

'Mikey' chimes back, 'Three-three, roger, cleared for take-off'. In less than a minute, 'Trim' and 'Mikey' are feet wet, (over water). On the prowl, and eager for a mid-air brawl, 'Trim' flexes the muscles of his Tomcat, pushing the throttle forward. 'Mikey' works his radar screen. His right hand grips the radar control stick on the radar panel. The right thumb rotates a dial on the stick, directing the radar beam, emitted from the jet's nose, up and down. Every few seconds he looks up and out into the world, whistling by at a cool 600 knots.

Meanwhilet, in another friendly TOPGUN F-14 two miles off their right beam, Lt Mark 'Action' Jackson and Lt Calvin 'Goose' Craig are going through similar manoeuvres.

PREVIOUS PAGE
Front left quarter view from the rear seat of an F-14, as Lt Kirk 'Willie' Williams in an F-16N turns to meet head-on a section combining another F-16N flown by Lt Bill 'Hack' McMasters and the F-14 piloted by Lt Jim 'Grits' Grimson

RIGHT
Capt Pat 'Kato' Cooke turns hard below the nose of the F-14, flown by Lt John 'Milt' Milton. Of the seven F-16Ns flown by NFWS, only one (BuNo 163269, '42') wears this olive green and pale grey paint scheme, selected by the Marine Corps

ABOVE

With condensation streaming from the forebody strakes of his F-16N, Capt Mant 'Gator' Hawkins pulls nine-G to defend against a combined attack by Lt Rob 'Ice' Ffield in an A-4 and Capt Thom 'T-Mac' McCarthy in a TF-16N

LEFT

The F-14 and the F-16N both go for the vertical. Traditionally, the aircraft that wins in this kind of manoeuvre is the one with the higher thrust/weight ratio, which would favour the F-16N

'What's up, 'Goose'?' muses 'Action'.

'Goose', normally quick on the humour draw, is silent. His luminescent radar screen glows with suspicion. Green symbols move from right to left, flashing on and off. 'Goose' steers the radar five degrees downward to confirm his discovery. The million-dollar apparatus processes and interprets the gossip-a TOPGUN F-16, simulating a MiG-29 Fulcrum. The lawn dart has yet to spot either F-14.

'Contact, on the nose, five degrees low, fifteen miles', signals 'Goose'.

Marine Corps Capt Pat 'Kato' Cooke, plugged snugly into his F-16N 'Viper', scans his radar upward five degrees. Flying alone in the ultimate video game taxes the conscious mind. Fighter pilots are guided by their on-board sensors. Lightning-fast, calculated reactions are the norm at altitude, while sifting through mounds of circumstantial evidence. The fighter who effectively uses his intuition has one more weapon with which to whip his enemy.

'Kato' suddenly feels uneasy after analyzing his radar screen. His reaction is immediate, he jams the gas pedal fully forward, dumping a hundred gallons of fuel into the engine. The afterburner kicks 'Kato' backward. The punch is noticeable, the extra power welcomed. 'Kato' shucks and jives during his ascent to 30,000 feet, shaking off the Tomcats' invisible clutches. He will need all the extra energy his 'Viper' can muster if he is to survive a backyard, no-holds-barred wrestling match with two Tomcats. 'Kato' keeps a close radar eye on the two F-14s closing in at over 1200 miles an hour and trying to get a radar lock onto the fast-moving 'Viper'.

Both 'Goose' and 'Mikey' try to line up their 'duck', but the fast and agile F-16 outmanoeuvres their attempted death grip.

View from the rear seat of a TA-4J flown by Capt Cletus 'Clete' Norris as it engages an F-16N flown by Lt Scott 'Sterno' Stearny

'Kato' talks out loud to hear his own thoughts. Mull them over. Crosscheck for errors. 'Viper' one contact, ten right, eight miles .Nose, six miles', he breathes loudly into his mike.

'Trim' and 'Action' follow the paths given by 'Mikey' and 'Goose'. The cockpit atmosphere lights up with energy and anticipation. The RIO's are talkative, animated, and eager to convey the latest info to their drivers.

The two Tomcats are now two miles from the 'Viper', closing in at 1800 feet per second. Less than six seconds until the first pass. 'Kato' pulls to the right, then hard left. He updates the approximate time he will pass the two F-14s – 'Three potatoes, two potatoes, one potato. . . ' And pulls harder on the stick, clutched in his right hand. The G indicator in his head up display (HUD) in front of his eyes climbs almost instantly. Two, four, six, eight Gs. Perspiration forcefully rushes down his face in sheets. The watch on his left wrist digs into his skin. His legs flatten out into large, jelly-filled rolls on the seat. Much of the air in his lungs has been squeezed out by the preternatural force. His heart struggles to send much-needed, oxygenated blood to his brain. Eight times the normal force of gravity at sea level saps 'Kato' of his strength. At the same time, evoking a flood of adrenalin that induces an atavistic aggression – the fight response. Hundreds of pounds of primal tiger, bearing down on its hapless prey. The flood allows 'Kato' to face this ultimate challenge.

As 'Kato' goes canopy to canopy with 'Action' and 'Goose' he frames the eyeballs-out look in 'Goose's' cobalt-blue eyes, which have lifted momentarily from his radar screen. Time seems to slow to an imperceptible crawl during the pass-time dilation. The phenomenon of time apparently slowing down, subsequently making all movements slow to a snail's pace. Theoretically, at 1800 feet

ABOVE

This is getting hairy! Forward view from 'Clete's' TA-4J as 'Sterno's' F-16N flashes across its nose. In principle there is a notional 500 ft (150 m) bubble around each aircraft, through which others will not pass for safety reasons. However, there are times...

RIGHT

View from the rear cockpit of an F-14 flown by Lt John 'Milt' Milton, in echelon port with Capt Pat 'Kato' Cooke in his F-16N formating on an F/A-18 flown by USMC Capt Chris 'Cooker' Cooke of VMFAT-101 'Sharpshooters'. Identified by the 'SH' tailcode, VMFAT-101 was previously the USMC Phantom II training unit, but in October 1987 relocated from MCAS Yuma, in Arizona, to El Toro, California, to re-equip with the Hornet. It is now the only USMC F/A-18 Fleet Replacement Squadron

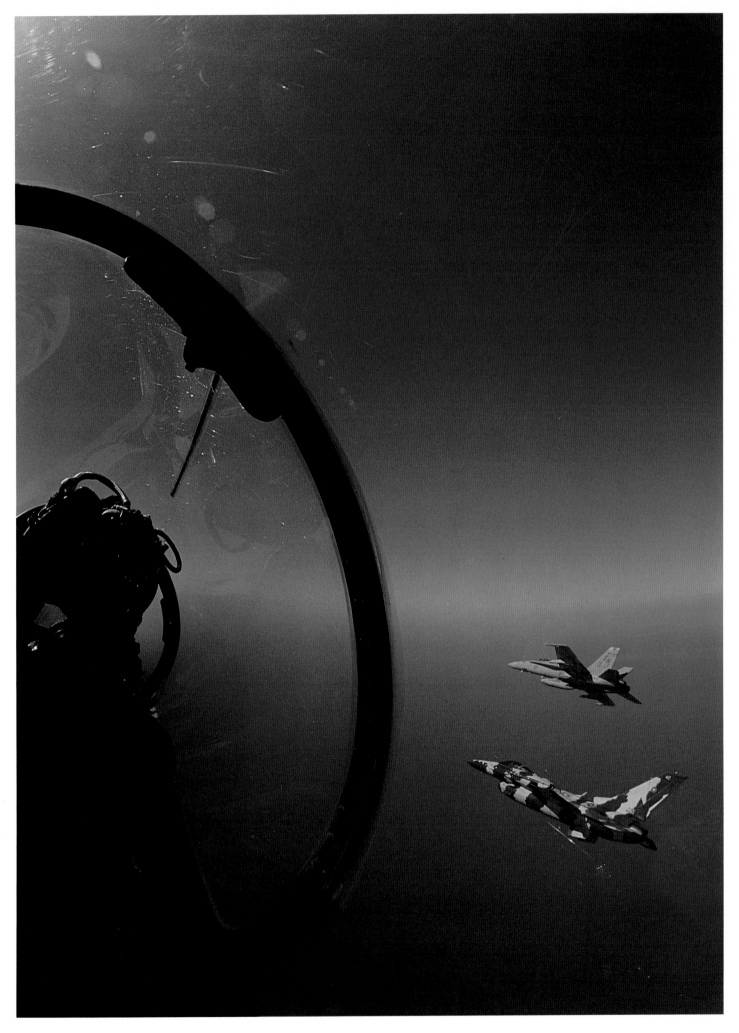

per second, any man will discern a passing object as a slightly greyish blur. The psychological paradox of time dilation defies theory, though, allowing both warriors to exchange glances of surprise, and of awe.

In the next millisecond, 'Action' is pulling behind 'Kato', who has turned on the G enough to out turn him. 'Kato' opts for a guns snap shot at 'Action's' helpless F-14, trying to keep an eye on the second F-14. 'Kato' leads the F-14, as would an experienced hunter shooting quail, and simulates firing off one hundred rounds of 20 mm bullets. 'Action' and 'Goose' pass through the imaginary bullet stream and swallow a dozen high-explosive bullets – they are dead.

"Viper', kill fighter, 25,000 feet, left turn', calls 'Kato'. The controller, Marine Corps Capt John 'Ajax' Neumann, in the TACTS trailer at Miramar, confirms 'Kato's' kill, 'Roger, 'Viper 'one, kill at two-five-oh'.

One of 'Ajax's' big jobs is kill removal. Documenting and confirming an aerial kill, then safely directing the 'dead' pilot out of the engagement. 'Action' and 'Goose' exit the arena, and climb to 30,000 feet. They orbit the flight, only five miles away. To the spectators, 'Trim' looks like a slow-moving fly, 'Kato' a large gnat, yet still much smaller than the fly he is battling. Both buzzing around each other, seemingly defying gravity. Despite excellent manoeuvring, the F-16 Viper cannot shake off the Tomcat, now cashing in on its initial advantage. 'Trim' and 'Mikey's' fly-sized Tomcat quickly reverses direction, lines up the 'Viper' on its nose, and then deftly delivers the coup de gras.

'Three-three locked, clear to engage. . Fox two,' announces 'Trim,' as his simulated heat seekers slam into the fleeing 'Viper', now bleeding energy during the seven-G turn.

'Roger, copy kill', calls 'Kato'.

ABOVE
Capt Cletus 'Clete' Norris in A-4F BuNo 154172, code '54', engages F-16N BuNo 163268, '02', flown by Lt Scott 'Sterno' Stearny

RIGHT
Two F-16Ns, flown by Lt Cdr Stan 'Steamer' O'Connor (now executive officer with VF-21 'Freelancers') and Capt Mant 'Gator' Hawkins, in the ascendant over the coast at San Clemente Island

An essential aid to NFWS operations is the ground-based TACTS (Tactical Air Combat Training System), which allows a controller in the TACTS trailer at NAS Miramar to guide and control an engagement, and then to arrange the removal of aircraft that are judged killed from the combat. In this illustration USMC Capt John 'Ajax' Neumann directs an engagement

RIGHT
One of several display modes available to the TACTS controller, this presentation synthesizes the forward view from an F-14 cockpit, with the horizon displayed as an oblique amber line, and the target aircraft clearly visible in the windscreen

BELOW RIGHT
The controller can alternatively select a bird's-eye view of the fight, in this case showing opposing aircraft and the path of an air-to-air missile

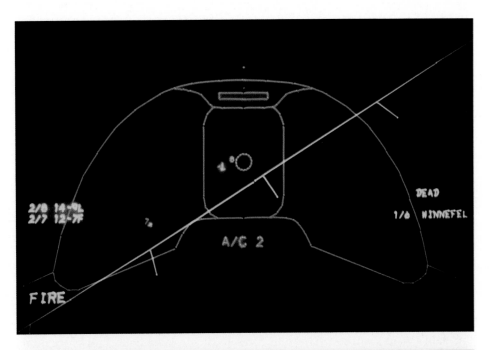

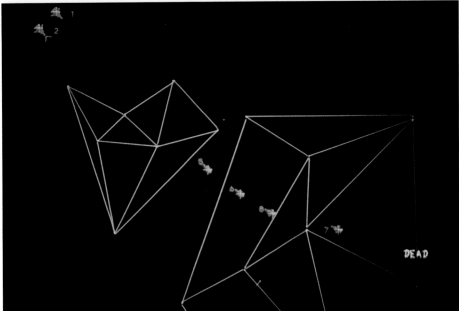

Having sanitized the area and successfully defended the home turf against the incoming MiG, 'Trim' comes back. 'Knock it off, guys', he calls and the trio join up for the flight home. In formation, each man visually checks the position and continuity of the other aircrafts' weapons, verifying that all's okay after the brawl. Then, it's time to head home.

On the ride back, the second Tomcat and the single 'Viper' fly in a loose delta formation off 'Trim' and 'Mikey'. Each man goes through a mental check-list of procedures to do just before, during and after landing at the Miramar ranch. The weather's fairly clear. Scattered clouds to the west at 12,000 feet. Sunset in five or six minutes. The clear skies mean a visual recovery. They will all use standard visual flight rules. Should the visibility get thick and muddy, the pilots will navigate solely by instruments and the voice of the Miramar control tower.

As the lead F-14 approaches the break near the runway, 'Mikey' pulls his face off the radar scope. 'Trim' pulls seven Gs in the 180-degree break turn. He then pulls his control stick back hard and to the left, throttle in full military power.

The high-pressure turn causes just enough drag to slow down the now-light air-craft in the pattern, and allow a smooth glide onto the runway.

'Trim' and 'Mikey' squeak a little Goodyear rubber into Miramar Highway, and taxy to Hangar One, home of TOPGUN. 'Action' and 'Goose', in the second F-14, and 'Kato', have also touched down, and are taxying to their respective parking spaces on the ramp outside Hangar One.

Now, it's time for a cold one to frost any depression after coming down from a ride on the ultimate roller coaster. And that's where the bartenders at the Miramar Officer's Club play their role in Naval Aviation. Bringing down, gingerly, those daring young men from their lofty perches. At the O Club, they decompress, releasing untold anger, anxiety, and restlessness. For those who've learned to take it all in their stride, the O Club is a social bastion for big boys who play with expensive toys. Each squadron seems to have its own coterie at the Club, where men of the same colourful patch congregate. They drink, they eat, they relax, seemingly all the while not noticing the other hundred or so hotshots just like them.

T S Eliot wrote about a character that enjoyed being around a lot of people, but didn't want them to talk to him. Perhaps these young fighter jocks are doing just that, feeding off the intense, emotional energy, emanating from each man and diffusing throughout the room, while, at the same time, not truly acknowledging the real source. Intense, aloof, arrogant, cocky, wholly self-sufficient, well-controlled men, bordering on the genius.

But, before the Club, the debrief. There, each man assembles in a room, and discusses the entire engagement. The debrief is where the pilots and RIO's constructively critique their work, and learn from their mistakes. Their aerial manoeuvres are scrutinized, all in the third person to prevent embarrassment or any sign of disrespect. No one at TOPGUN points fingers. Even when 'Trim' discusses his eight-G left turn that ended up in his gunning the F-16, he says, 'the Tomcat went into the merge with a good visual on the 'Viper'. The Tomcat pulled hard left, about eight Gs, got inside the turn radius of the F-16, and took a guns snap shot at about 800 feet. Kill one F-16', he concludes respectfully. This type of dialogue among the men continues for about an hour, depending on the complexity of the engagement. No question goes unanswered. All 'spaghetti' trails, the intertwined lines on the briefing board that denote the flight paths of the engaged fighters, are drawn as accurately as possible. The pilot leading the debrief takes care to ensure that they all address one or two key issues of the fight. Subsequent mistakes often follow the one or two big ones, so the men don't necessarily sweat the 'little' things. Usually, the small mistakes will be repaired by working out the big goofs.

Optimally, the debrief will offer one or more useful techniques to avoid the same, or similar, mistakes next time. Finally, the leader of the debrief will relate the lessons learned to the objective of the hop, which was studied in the briefing before the flight. Thoroughness is expected at TOPGUN.

'Kato', eager to engage Wednesday night's guests at the Club – young, eligible females from off base – looks at the motley bunch, in dire need of thirst aid, and announces stoically, 'O Club'.

RIGHT
Sunburst shot of a TOPGUN F-16N and TF-16N on combat air patrol (CAP); the single seater is piloted by Lt Bill 'Hack' McMasters, whilst the 'twin tub' is crewed by Maj Billy 'Stump' Miles and Lt Calvin 'Goose' Craig

PREVIOUS PAGE

Rear quarter shot of a Hornet from VMFAT-101, flown by Capt Chris 'Cooker' Cooke. The 'SH 132' code identifies this as F/A-18C BuNo 163709. Interestingly, the standard reference works indicate that VMFAT-101 aircraft bear no unit badge, but this example clearly has a toned-down insignia on the vertical tail

LEFT

Three Marine Corps pilots head back to NAS Miramar after an air combat training exercise, led by Capt Pat 'Kato' Cooke in F-16N '42' (BuNo 163269), with Capt Bob 'Jeckyll' Cotterell on his port wing in F-16N '40' (BuNo 163273) and Capt Chris 'Cooker' Cooke on his starboard wing in F/A-18C 'SH 132' (BuNo 163709)

ABOVE
The Marines' F-16N in one-off camouflage, flown by Capt Pat 'Kato' Cooke. The NFWS unit badge on the vertical tail shows a MiG (possibly a MiG-21 with a certain artistic licence) as seen through a gunsight, with the pipper squarely on the central fuselage

RIGHT
Dogfight over, Lt Dave 'Shooter' Vanderschoot turns his F-16N away over the Pacific. What appears to be an AIM-9 on his starboard wingtip is in fact a data-pod that feeds information to the Tactical Air Combat Training System (TACTS) trailer on the ground

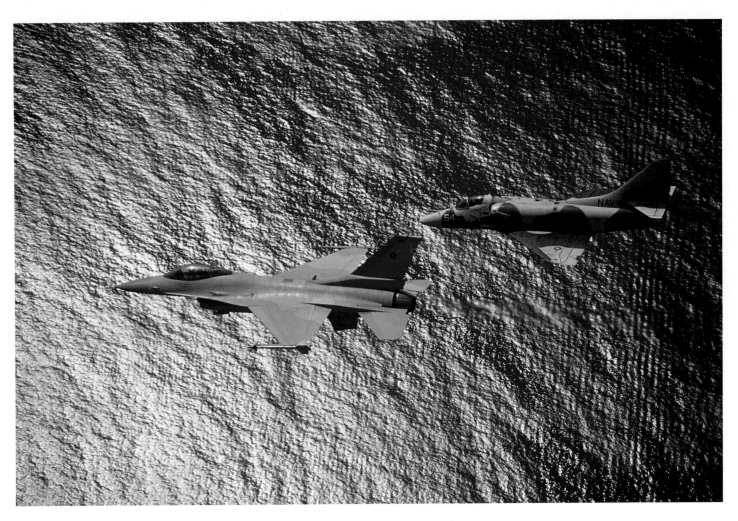

Captains Pat 'Kato' Cooke and Bob 'Jeckyll' Cotterell in F-16Ns '42' (BuNo 163269) and '40' (BuNo 163273) go 'feet dry' as they turn over the shoreline of San Clemente Island

ABOVE
A pleasing study of two TOPGUN aircraft heading out over the Pacific to dogfight in a training area. Lt Bill 'Hack' McMasters is flying the A-4F (BuNo 154172), while (9100 aircraft later!) F-16N '45' (BuNo 163272) is piloted by Capt Bob 'Jeckyll' Cotterell

OVERLEAF
On approach to NAS Miramar, this F-16N (BuNo 163272), flown by Lt Bill 'Hack' McMasters, provides a good illustration of the very effective air superiority camouflage scheme applied to all but two of the Navy's 'Vipers'

ABOVE
*Two NFWS 'Vipers' on combat air patrol: Marine Major Billy 'Stump' Miles in F-16N '43'
(BuNo 163270), and Lt Calvin 'Goose' Craig and Lt Bill 'Hack' McMasters in TF-16N '46'
(BuNo 163279). The two-seater requires a centreline 300 US gallon (1136 litre) tank to offset
its higher weight and reduced internal capacity, the TF-16N holding only 5659 lbs (2566 kgs)
compared to the 6846 lbs (3104 kgs) of the single-seater*

RIGHT
*A mixed bag of NFWS aircraft in formation over San Clemente Island, with Lt Cdr Stan
'Steamer' O'Connor flying the lead F-16N, Capt Mant 'Gator' Hawkins in the second F-16N,
Lt Rob 'Ice' Ffield in the lead A-4 and Lt Greg 'Hoser' Hansen in the second Skyhawk*

*The pale grey and blue camouflage of the
F-16N is effective against both sky and cloud.
This example, '43' (BuNo 163270), is being
flown by Lt Bill 'Hack' McMasters*

Waiting for 'trade' – an F-14 flown by Lt Tom 'Trim' Downing and Lt Calvin 'Goose' Craig, and with the wings in the fully swept position, leads an F-16N flown by Lt Bill 'Hack' McMasters

LEFT

The F-16N is quite a lively aircraft, being basically a Block 30 F-16C (ie, with the more powerful F110 in place of the F100), but with weight reduced by the deletion of the gun and ASPJ provisions. These 26 aircraft were built in the period 1987-88, and this example, '45' (BuNo 163272) was the fifth off the line

ABOVE

A Grumman F-14 with wings at an intermediate setting, flown by Lts Tom 'Trim' Downing and Calvin 'Goose' Craig. The strange excrescence under the nose currently houses an infrared search and track (IRST) sensor, a small anti-collision beacon and a transmitting antenna for the Sanders ALQ-126 jammer. The IRST takes the place of the earlier Northrop AXX-l TCS (television camera set), which was used for the long-range identification of airborne and surface targets. The F-14D can take both the TCS and IRST

There's a lot of sky out there, and any minute now there could be a NFWS instructor claiming a kill on this TA-4J. The wide angle of the lens gives depth of focus, but also distorts the Skyhawk's cropped delta planform. Note the two rows of vortex generators, the front row delaying leading-edge separation, and the rear row helping to maintain aileron effectiveness

Flaps down and engines smoking slightly, TOPGUN A-4s flown by Capt Cletus 'Clete' Norris and Lt Dave 'Shooter' Vanderschoot close in on the C-2A 'camera-ship'

Close enough? Full frontal view of A-4F '54' (BuNo 154172) flown by 'Clete'. The photograph demonstrates the use of a centreline stores pylon with sway-bracing, and the fact that the Skyhawk's intakes do restrict pilot view in the rear hemisphere to some extent, though clearly less than in the case of the AV-8 Harrier series

As 'Clete' breaks away, the suction over the leading-edge pulls the slats open. Although these automatic slats represent a minimal servicing task, there were stories in the Skyhawk's early days of an occasional asymmetric extension, leading to an unplanned snap-roll

Airbrakes out, showing a good example of toned-down national markings, Skyhawk '53' holds station with the photographic aircraft. The configuration of the flight refuelling probe is clearly seen, and it is perhaps surprising that the Pratt & Whitney J52 engine swallows the disturbed flow from this probe without protest

OVERLEAF
One of TOPGUN's F-14 Tomcats over the Sierra Nevadas in February 1992. Despite what was said in the TOP GUN film, the F-14A is far from being the ultimate dogfighting aircraft, but NFWS has to operate a small number of these fighters to substitute for students' machines that go unserviceable and to broaden the threat spectrum

PREVIOUS PAGE
Nosing up over the ridge-line, this NFWS F-14 is crewed by Lts Tom 'Trim' Downing and Calvin 'Goose' Craig. Since the Tomcat made its first flight on 21 December 1970, its performance is hardly representative of modern fighter technology, but its radar still provides a useful edge over most combat aircraft, and its cockpit workload still generates a challenge for ambitious instructors

LEFT
Rearward view from the NFWS F-14 back seat as it pulls six-G, with condensation trails streaming from the wingtips. The ejection handles over the photographer's bone-dome provide a reminder of how aircrew traditionally 'stepped outside' with Martin-Baker seats, but most escapes are now made with crotch-handles

Going home, TF-16N '46' (BuNo 163279), crewed by Lts Scott 'Sterno' Stearney and Pete 'Skids' Matthews, pops the brakes and drops the lot as they formate off the starboard tip of the TA-4J, flown by Maj Billy 'Stump' Miles

OVERLEAF
A wide-angle lens can do terrible things to a beautiful aeroplane, in this instance F-16N '45' (BuNo 163272) as it turns on finals at NAS Miramar

Chapter five
Support Missions

'The man behind the man, behind the man. The unsung hero. Being a member of an elite organization, known throughout the world as 'numero uno', my recipe for success is very basic: stay in school, don't do drugs and believe in thy self!' – Yeoman Second Class Tony Berkel, Administrative Support

If the heart and soul of TOPGUN are the instructors and students, then the backbone surely is the support personnel. Literally hundreds of man-hours go into each hour that a single TOPGUN jet is aloft. While much of the direct work comes from maintenance personnel, working on and around the aircraft, the paperwork, filing, procuring, selling, writing, discussing, gathering and interpreting is done primarily by non-aviation people.

'The sailors and marines that dedicate themselves to administrative and maintenance support have been the backbone of TOPGUN. Their selfless devotion to duty does not always gain the recognition it deserves, but every pilot and RIO knows that the effort of these individuals is directly responsible for the thoroughness and ease at which we as instructors are able to accomplish the mission of TOPGUN'. – Marine Corps Major Billy 'Stump' Miles, Operations Officer

The Administration Department, headed by Lt Cdr Jeff Taylor, co-ordinates all administrative details of TOPGUN. It is tasked with handling correspondence prepared by the Commanding Officer and Executive Officer, ensuring that it conforms to Navy standards.

Adminstration maintains extensive files on Navy regulations, orders, and non-technical publications. And, quite often, the Adminstration Department handles daily requests for tours by local, state and federal government officials, private company executives, public and civic groups, colleges, high schools, elementary schools and the general public.

Particularly rewarding are visits by young and terminally ill children. They seem to be really in tune and alert to the goings on at TOPGUN. And they are especially animated when they walk onto the flightline and step inside one of TOPGUN's A-4s, F-14s or F-16s. Lt Cdr Taylor and company also reward the visitors with personalized call signs and a leather TOPGUN flight patch, with their name and new call sign imprinted in Navy gold. Public visits do take a lot

of extra time, but TOPGUN personnel are richly rewarded emotionally by the appreciation expressed by the visitors.

'One of my more memorable experiences was when the 'Make a Wish Foundation' brought about thirty terminally ill children from New Zealand to visit the squadron. It was very uplifting to see the sheer pleasure it brought to these children just to meet a few pilots and see our jets'.– Kathy Moore, Executive Secretary

Other visitors to TOPGUN include members of the media. Lt Bill 'Hack' McMasters heads the Media Office and, along with Mr Greg Palmore, an audio-visual specialist, and other TOPGUN personnel, often escorts these journalists around the squadron.

'About two weeks after I arrived at TOPGUN, I was tasked to drop off someone at the San Diego Airport. That went okay, but I got lost and ended up at the Tijuana border, which is in the opposite direction from Miramar. Everyone now tells me to file a flight plan when I attempt to go somewhere'.– Yeoman Third Class Teresa Sheppard, Legal Yeoman, Administration Department

Some journalists are lucky enough to climb aboard a TOPGUN jet and experience a once-in-a-lifetime ride in one of the Navy's most lethal weapons. The majority, though, are rewarded with a well-guided tour of the School or a particular area at TOPGUN.

'Every year, TOPGUN has a little party in the hangar, and Santa arrives in a jet. Well, last year I had the pleasure of helping to paint Santa's cheeks a rosy colour. We put lipstick on Lt Bill 'Hack' McMasters' cheeks, but he didn't care too much for it. Actually, he thought he looked like a sissy. We wanted to get a full view of his outfit, so we ended up taking him into the women's bathroom, so none of the children would see him. After fixing him up, his pants fell down, revealing some very colourful surfer shorts. Needless to say, we all had a good laugh about that. But the best part was that when he was going to his jet his pants fell down again! I must admit that last year's Santa was the most hilarious I've ever seen!' – CT03 Cheryl Gray, Cryptologic Technician Officer

The Media Office, equipped with state-of-the-art recording, dubbing, and sound-analyzing equipment, also produces videos for instructors ' lectures and briefings, and for the extensive TOPGUN video library. At any given moment, Mr Greg Palmore is tending several different recorders and listening to the latest Anita Baker song on cable television. If anyone can do several jobs at once – very effectively – it's Mr Palmore.

While most non-flying personnel at TOPGUN have an open-door policy, there is one small community, tucked away in a corner of the TOPGUN complex, with secured doors. No windows. No view to the outside world. The sign on the door, the big red sign, reads 'SECRET'.

Lt Tom 'Clubber' Lang and Mr Mel 'Spine Ripper' Horowitz, in the Intelligence Department, sit behind locked doors, gathering yards of data. They not only gather intelligence information, but interpret information about the latest threats to the Navy's aerial warfare defence and early warning system.

Clubber' and 'Spine Ripper' continually update the most likely threats, and convey their news to the Training Department at TOPGUN, in charge of designing the school's syllabus. They also communicate with members of the intelligence community, co-ordinating and directing aspects of tactical intelligence.

'In my former job, I served as the Intelligence Department Head for a Navy Special Warfare unit, and deployed to Saudi Arabia for – in that capacity. I thought that the pace over there was as high as it could get. However, the pace

PREVIOUS PAGE
Flying the thing is only one element of the total man-hours. In this picture TOPGUN servicing personnel prepare to scrub down a Skyhawk. Interesting design features include the A-4's rudder, which (to save weight) was given a central 'skin' with uncovered half-ribs. Very few Skyhawks used in the adversary role retain the fin-mounted ECM pods

RIGHT
A closer look at the back end of A-4F '55' (BuNo 154173) shows the unique rudder to better effect. Proof that the widely acclaimed Ed Heinemann didn't get it completely right the first time is provided by the 'coal-scuttle' fairing over the jetpipe, which alleviated problems associated with the excessive decrease in cross-section area toward the rear end

of activity since being given the Maritime Air Threat lecture at TOPGUN has increased geometrically. In this capacity, I have the luxury of examining problems in depth, and calling on a wide variety of intelligence sources for the latest information. That, in turn, allows me to bring the highest levels of expertise to bear on questions like the Maritime Air Threat, and get that info out to the fleet. The fleet is what matters. What counts is intelligence that can be used for and by the guys who get shot at'.— Lt Tom 'Clubber' Lang, Intelligence Officer

And should anyone at TOPGUN violate a safety or security code, 'Spine Ripper' is only a step away, his meat-cleaver sized hands around their necks.

'All staff instructors fully appreciate the seriousness of maintaining security integrity of classified material, and the circumstances if violated'. — Mr Mel 'Spine Ripper' Horowitz, Special Security Officer

The Maintenance shop supports air operations by maintaining and repairing all aircraft assigned to TOPGUN. Cdr Mel Prior oversees the duties of all aircraft maintenance personnel, who stow, issue, and keep track of all supplies and materials related to flying. Personnel under his command inspect and maintain everything in the A-4 and TA-4 trainer. Day and night crews work so that maintenace is ongoing for at least 18 hours each weekday. At any given hour, men and women are in the maintenance shops or hangar with their heads inside the internal compartments of the aircraft. They, too, look for obvious and not-so-obvious wear and tear, breaks, cracks, bends, leaks, loose joints and, in general, signs of fatigue.

Although the A-4 is 25 years older than the F-16, the Skyhawk has enjoyed a reputation of sturdiness and reliability – unlike the heavily fatigued 'Vipers', many of which have been grounded over the past two years.

The Maintenance shop, directly supervised by Lt Peggy D'Haene and Master Chief Jay Hogan, employs plane captains, who are assigned a particular aircraft. Each male and female plane captain oversees the day-to-day operations of an A-4. Although budget cuts have reduced manpower, the Line Division, supervised by Petty Officer Don Kidd, has maintained an impressively high mission-ready status. During the day on the flightline or in the hangar, Petty Officer Kidd oversees his troops, always keeping a step ahead of the next potential mishap. He keeps his men and women within his keen peripheral vision, while communicating on his 'walkie talkie'. He never stops moving. Petty Officer Kidd's paternal instinct and devotion to the young sailors under his aegis create a very comfortable work environment.

'When I left for boot camp in 1987, I was scared to be leaving my family and to adventure into the unknown. Since I've been at TOPGUN, I consider this my second home'. – AMSAN Paul T Richards, Leading Airman Daycheck Line All supervisors keep a close eye on their men and women, ensuring that TOPGUN aircraft meet the high standards set forth by the Navy, especially in the face of adversity.

'Due to military budget cuts, our manpower has drastically been reduced. The Line Division has shown through camaraderie, dedication, professionalism

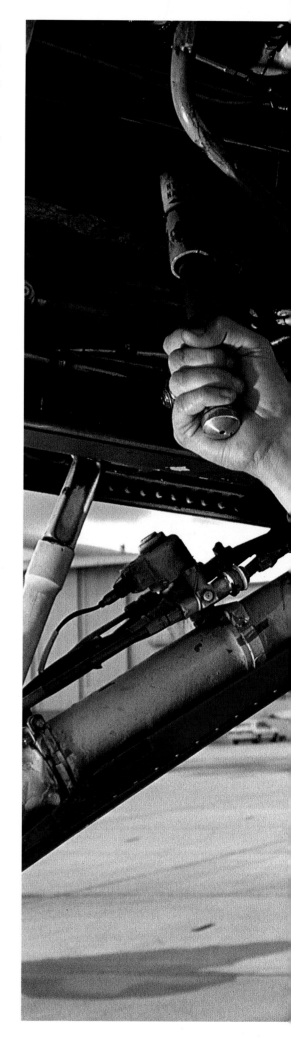

Navy AME1 Bob Relph performs routine servicing on a Skyhawk. Judging by his patches, Relph came to NFWS from VF-51 'Screaming Eagles', a small detachment of which was based at Hangar One in 1985 for the filming of the Tom Cruise 'epic' Top Gun. VF-51 also claim to have been the first US Navy unit to intercept Backfire bombers and armed MiG-23 Flogger and Su-15 Flagon fighters

Navy AMEl Bob Relph checks the cockpit of the A-4. His right shoulder patch indicates that he has friendly relations with early warning squadron VAW-110, currently operating E-2C Hawkeyes and C-2A Greyhounds out of NAS Miramar

ABOVE

Keeping the jets in the air, the US Navy is supported by contractor personnel– in this case a representative from General Dynamics is carrying out a preflight check on an F-14A at Miramar. The corporation is the contractor responsible for certain maintenance activities on all aircraft operated by the NFWS

and perseverance that we can overcome any obstacle to get the job done with the utmost military bearing. We are all enthusiastic to uphold the mission of TOPGUN and the US Navy. As long as there are top performers like the Line in the military, there will always be a free country in which to live'. – AMSAN Dave Trainer, Plane Captain

The Parachute Rigger (PR) shop in Hangar One also maintains a high degree of integrity, mission-preparedness and morale among its men and women. The PR's procure, inspect, maintain, and stow all flight gear worn and used by the TOPGUN pilots. Parachute Riggers PR1 Ed Mazuda, PR2 Bill Rodebaugh, and PR3 Ed Rollins produce the leather and gold name plates for flight suits and jackets, sew up rips and tears in flight gear and parachutes, design and sew leather covers for flight helmets, and leather covered knee boards for pilots, and clean and inspect all flight equipment. Sharing the same area with the Maintenance folks fosters a lively, gregarious atmosphere. The work is tough, the men and women are highly professional. But they seem to realize the importance of not taking themselves too seriously. They have fun at their work. They laugh and joke and kid around with each other. They make TOPGUN their home away from home. Thus, the arduous task of flying in a high-performance jet is assuaged by the selfless dedication to duty of all support personnel at TOPGUN.

'I feel that my role here is very important, because if the pilots don't get qualified, and something happens to the pilot while flying, a lot of people could be in some major trouble. So while my role may look simple on the outside, NATOPS/Safety is the heart and soul of TOPGUN'. – Yeoman Third Class Eric Earl Ellis, NATOPS

ABOVE
The golden rule in avoiding terminal injury from electrical sources is to work with the right hand, while keeping the left hand firmly in one's pocket, thus minimising the current experienced by the heart. This character is playing it doubly safe by keeping both hands in the air'!

RIGHT
Contractor personnel perform checks on Grumman F-14 '32' at NAS Miramar. The aft-hinged canopy clearly demands a more powerful actuator than in the case of a side-mounted hood, but may provide advantages in terms of in-flight jettison

OVERLEAF
Back to the hangar' The aviators are installed in their cockpits, but the engineers have a burned-out flight computer on their hands

ABOVE

Send it back to the maker! Civilian contractors examine the burned-out computer from an F-14 Tomcat

RIGHT

Two civilian contractors preflight a TOPGUN F-14. Undercarriage bays traditionally provide convenient access to a variety of aircraft systems, especially hydraulic components. The apertures seen in the top of the intake duct are spill doors, provided to dump excess air overboard rather than spill it around the intake lips

ABOVE

'Fire up number three! On the ground, with its wings fully swept, the Tomcat looks somewhat ungainly. However, in-flight the ability to vary leading-edge sweep from 20 to 68 degrees provides an outstanding combination of time-on-station, slow approach speed and low wave drag. On the deck, the wings can be overswept to 75 degree to minimise parking area requirements

RIGHT

A pool of fuel leaked from the aircraft catches fire during start-up. Most aircraft (both military and civil) have problems with fuel leaks, hence the popularity of bonded composite structures such as the AV-8B wing, with the minimum of holes for rivets and bolts

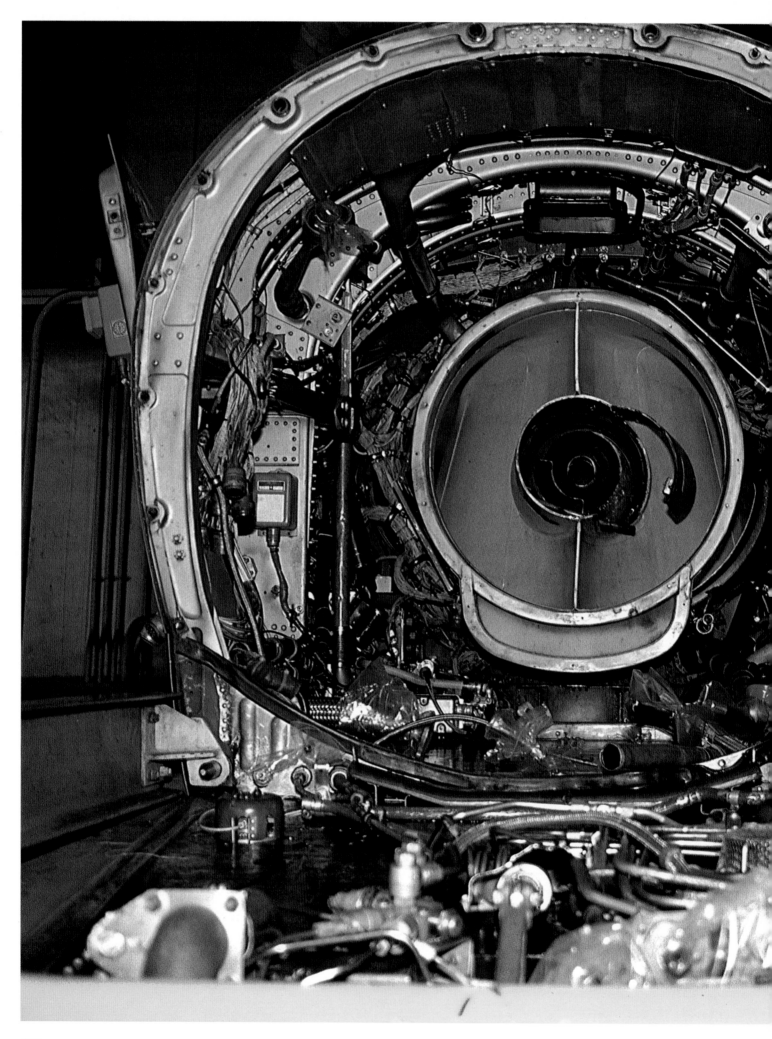

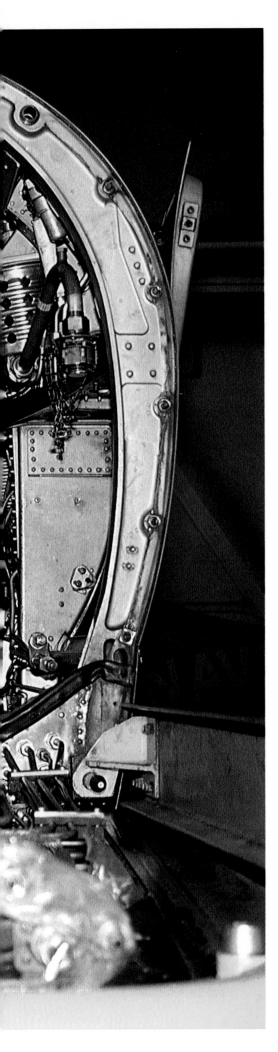

ABOVE

'Hang a left, and the runway is that 10,000 ft (3000 m) piece of concrete. Have a nice day'

LEFT

What is left of an A-4 fuselage when the rear end is taken off and the engine removed. This form of engine change came in with the F-80, F-84, F-86 etc, and is not popular with groundcrew as it involves breaking all the services to the rear end. A much better approach is seen in the F/A-18, in which the engines are simply dropped out through large apertures left by stress-bearing access panels

ABOVE

USMC Maj Tony 'Spike' Valentino prepares to celebrate the successful conclusion of his final flight with the NFWS

RIGHT

'Spike's' tour with TOPGUN is celebrated in traditional fashion with a bucket of water, emptied over the head of the pilot as he climbs down from the cockpit after his last sortie with the school

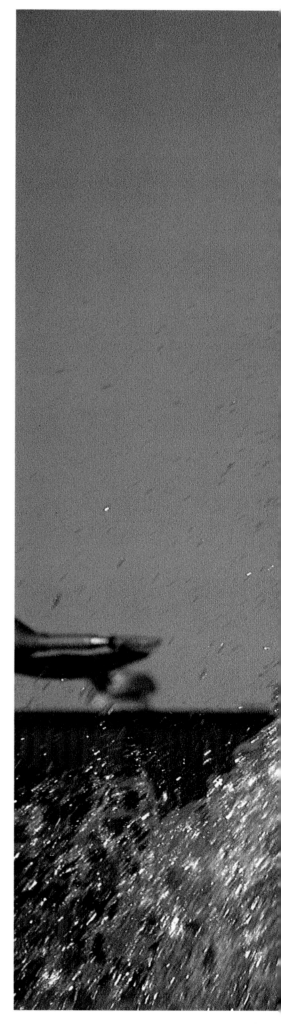

ABOVE
Maj Billy 'Stump' Miles congratulates 'Spike' on the completion of his tour of duty, while in the background an F-16N is prepared for its next sortie

RIGHT
The fuel truck, loaded with highly flammable JP5 jet fuel, makes its rounds prior to the afternoon flying, while TA-4J '57' waits for its next assignment. Traditionally, British forces described their fuel as 'inflammable', but the American version 'flammable' is now widely accepted in the UK

ABOVE

Parachute Rigger PR1 Ed Muzada carries out repairs on an F-16N survival vest prior to a sortie. Despite its title, the Parachute Rigger shop is responsible not just for parachutes, but for all flight-gear, including helmets and the leather-covered knee-boards on which aircrew make their notes

RIGHT

Mr Mel 'Spine Ripper' Horowitz, special security officer, in his office in the NFWS Intelligence Department, the most secure part of the TOPGUN establishment

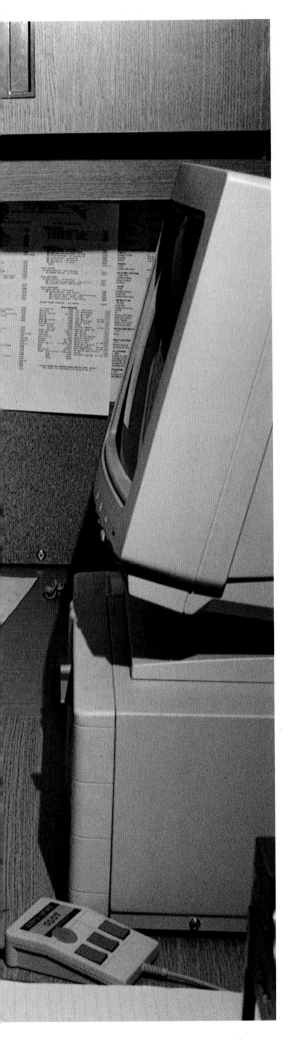

ABOVE LEFT

Scott Downing prepares the flight schedule for the next day

LEFT

Navy Lt Peggy D'Haene, seen here at her computer, supervises the NFWS maintenance shop with the assistance of Master Chief Jay Hogan and the various plane captains, who are assigned to individual aircraft

ABOVE RIGHT

One lady with whom a lot of young women would like to change places: TOPGUN executive secretary Kathy Moore

Chapter six
Future of TOPGUN
A Commitment to Naval Aviation Excellence

by Vice Admiral Richard M Dunleavy,
Assistant Chief of Naval Operations, Air Warfare

The creation of the Navy Fighter Weapons School, and its impact on the air war over Southeast Asia, is well documented. TOP GUN, the film, captured the public's imagination throughout the world. Often overlooked are the years of hard work and sacrifice that have maintained 'The Gun School' at the forefront of fighter tactics, technology and instruction.

Over the years, threat systems have evolved dramatically to include three-dimensional radars, high-speed surface-to-air missiles (SAMs), deadly fighters, and dense anti-air artillery (AAA) that are co-ordinated and integrated with modern computers. Soviet and western sales of combat equipment have given third world countries first-world militaries.

No longer can fighter pilots be successful simply through 'seat-of-the-pants' flying. Today's combat aircrews need to have an in-depth knowledge of high-tech systems and thorough familiarity with complex power projection tactics, in addition to the aggressiveness, lightning reflexes, and steely flight discipline that they have in common with the aviation heroes of the past.

The TOPGUN staff maintains close contact with The Naval Strike Warfare Center, Marine Aviation Weapons Training Squadron, US intelligence agencies, fleet squadrons, and the US Air Force Fighter Weapons School in order to gather and share the latest tactical information. Thanks to their tireless efforts, US Navy fighter aviation has made dramatic improvements in the past decade. From the Vietnam days of rear-quarter air-to-air missile tactics, with sporadic and autonomous SAM and AAA defences, they have lead the evolution of tactics and training into the beyond-visual-range missile arena, which includes threats to US forces from sophisticated, integrated air defences. The professionalism and lethality of Navy and Marines aircrew in *Desert Storm* was due, in part, to the tradition of excellence and realism in training that is TOPGUN's hallmark.

As we face an uncertain future of regional conflicts, US military reductions, and a proliferation of combat hardware around the globe, it is the superior training of our warriors that will again provide the decisive advantage. The Navy Fighter Weapons School will certainly keep Naval Aviation 'the best of the best'.

PREVIOUS PAGE

There's an opening for you at TOPGUN, but only if you're good enough to fill the shoes of men such as Lt Scott 'Sterno' Stearney, to whom A-4F '50' (BuNo 155000) was assigned

LEFT

A nicely composed shot of A-4s flown by Lts Rob 'Ice' Ffield and Greg 'Hoser' Hansen, as seen from a TF-16N flown by Capt Thom 'T-Mac' McCarthy, somewhere over the Pacific

ABOVE

Maj Billy 'Stump' Miles and 'Lt Calvin 'Goose' Craig, en route for action in TF-16N '46' (BuNo 163279)

RIGHT
Bank and pull! View from the rear seat of a TA-4J as the pilot prepares to generate a very positive load factor

ABOVE
Rear-quarter shots are seldom flattering, but General Dynamics' F-16N manages to look attractive enough as it banks away from the 'camera-ship' at sunset

ABOVE
The clean lines of the Grumman F-14 are well illustrated as this Tomcat makes a flapless, non-afterburning take-off with the 'camera-ship'

RIGHT
Perfect for the cover, this image combines F-16Ns, a sunburst effect and some very attractive clouds

ABOVE
Skyhawk at sunset, in this case A-4F '51' (BuNo 154209). The A-4F was the final major variant built for the US Navy, some 146 examples being manufactured by Douglas. It is differentiated from the A-4E by the Doppler bulge under the nose, but primarily by a large avionics fairing over the fuselage; the fairing has been removed from all TOPGUN Skyhawks to save weight. Aside from visible differences, the A-4E has the 8500-lb (3855 kg) J52-P6 engine, whereas the A-4F was built with the 9300-lb (4220 kg) J52-P8A, and about 100 A-4Fs were retrofitted with 11,000-lb (4990 kg) J52-P-501s

LEFT
The F-14 turns over the Sierra Nevada mountain range. A total of 157 F-14As were delivered to the US Navy before production switched in FY86 to the F-14A(Plus), now redesignated F-14B. In FY88 production switched again to the F-14D. Both the F-14B and D have the more powerful F110-GE-400 engines in place of the original Pratt & Whitney TF30s, and the F-14D has the improved Hughes APG-71 radar in place of the original AWG-9, plus other avionic improvements. There have been 70 F-14Bs built (including 32 remanufactured A-models) and 37 F-14Ds, all new-built

Chapter seven
Shooting TOPGUN

T alk to me, 'Goose', says a cocky, overconfident Lieutenant Pete 'Maverick' Mitchell in the blockbuster film, TOP GUN. Their F-14 Tomcat, 20 tons of fire-spitting, rocket-slinging hell with wings, picks up the telltale sign of multiple bogies.

'Goose' peers into his 115-square inches of green 'crystal ball', the Tomcat's AWG-9 radar screen, and barks, 'Roger, I got' em. Contact 20 left, 30 miles'. The two-storey high drama played awesomely in front of me at a theatre in Long Beach, California – 26 different performances during the summer of 1986. More than fifty hours' and one hundred dollars' worth of pure, high-octane intoxication. How could I not be enraptured by the danger and romance of fighter aviation?

Since I was a boy, I'd watched my father, an ex-Air Force F-4 driver, take off tyre-scorched runways in his camouflaged F-4 Phantom II. I missed him desperately during his two-year tour in South-east Asia in 1968 and 1969. He bombed North Vietnam and I bombed third-grade maths. Living in Germany, many an afternoon I sat in his high-tech cockpit. Right hand on the control stick, left on the throttle, I imagined flying through a miasma of flak, smoke, and white-hot sky. I sat there, wearing my thick, Perrier-bottle-bottom, black-frame glasses, dreaming the impossible. Or so I thought.

Surely TOPGUN rekindled my deep-seated, repressed dream to become a fighter pilot . To scream across diaphanous blue skies at Mach two, not a care in the world below. But here I was, finishing a Master's Degree in Marine Biology, far from flying in a Lear Jet, much less a high-performance fighter jet. Don't ask how it happened, it just did. Within a year after seeing TOP GUN, I was strapping on an F-4E Phantom II, similar to the jet in which my father flew. Again, I don't know how it all came to be, but that first flight, even though we aborted due to afterburner failure, led to another, and another.

During those first few flights in the US Air Force's A-7, F-4, F-15, F-16, and KC-135, and the US Navy F-16N at TOPGUN, I developed my aerial photography skills from ground zero. Not having photographed before, I was reinventing the wheel many times over, taking beautiful– and not-so-beautiful– shots of those majestic machines, and often publishing photos in books, magazines and newspapers.

All of my efforts paid off in 1991, when I signed a contract to photograph and write my own book featuring TOPGUN. It took one and a half years of planning, dozens of letters, phone calls, meetings, and test shoots. Then, almost two years since I'd first flown at TOPGUN in the F-16N, I climbed aboard a TOPGUN legend, the A-4 Skyhawk, pulled on 30 years of aviation history, and leaped off the right runway into a cool, California afternoon.

Navy Lieutenant Bill 'Hack' McMasters flew us over some of southern California's most breathtaking vistas, while I reacquainted myself with my cameras and, in general, how to shoot from the back seat of a very fast-moving platform that pitched and rolled and climbed and tumbled, often under six-plus Gs. The added stressors fuelled my enthusiasm and excitement and I quickly adapted to the aerial stage once again. While 'Hack' scorched up a rocky valley upside down, I practiced handling each camera, shooting out the left and right side of the scratched, plexiglass canopy. 'Hack' climbed for high altitude to gain energy, then whipped the stick sideways, and then back hard. We pulled five Gs as we dived toward the satin Pacific, 15,000 feet below. Our bodies suddenly weighed five times more. My camera, ten pounds on land (a comfortable, familiar one-G environment) metamorphosed into fifty pounds of bobcat, claws erect. The film canister I was loading into the hefty, hungry camera weighed more than a McDonald's quarter-pound cheeseburger. By the end of that flight, I had relearned all the tricks I had invented over the past few years. And I had set the stage for some spectacular aerial photography.

Shooting the aerials was relatively easy, although physically exhausting. Flying twice a day, and then spending many hours editing a previous day's slides, all I wanted to do afterward was fall into a deep sleep. The ground shots were more challenging, mainly because of logisitics – just finding people to shoot, moving aircraft around, etc. Donna, my wife, helped edit the work, and set up ground and aerial shots, and typed the manuscript. She also flew aboard a C-2 Greyhound, courtesy of VAW-110, and along with a crew member photographed my shooting an E-2 and two TOPGUN A-4s. Her expert assistance in photographing, and in other areas of the book, assuaged the physical and mental pain of doing the entire project alone. Not impossible, but tough.

Planning a jet-fighter photography shoot takes a few brain cells. Donna and I are lucky. We are both thinkers. We both sat down months in advance of my flying in the A-4, F-14 and F-16, and both of us in the C-2, and typed a detailed, fifteen-page 'wish list' of possible aerial and ground photographs. Then, we decided which ones to shoot first, and when and where to photograph them. Obviously, we listed many more than we could possibly shoot. And, sometimes the ones we later shot seemed redundant and a bit too similar to previous images, even if the background was different. But the apparent shortcomings of the project did not daunt us in any way. They only prompted us to think harder and more creatively.

Physical Considerations

Photography, in general, can be done almost by anyone, regardless of physical condition. The list of shooters is long and impressive. To illustrate the difficulty of shooting from a high-performance military aircraft, let's inject a little discomfort. Dress our photographer in 30 lbs of helmet, parachute harness, survival vest, G-suit, flight suit, flight gloves, flight boots and, just for show, a flowing white silk scarf. And make it all fit like a pair of wing-tip shoes, one size too small. Fresh off the press. Hard as a rock. Flexible as plate glass. The resulting claustrophobia, most likely, will pare down our list of photographers somewhat,

sending most back to their studios and wedding rehearsal dinners. Our scenario is, perhaps, somewhat similar to photographing sitting ducks on a calm pond. But our photographer is inappropriately attired in a space suit. Moreover, he no longer has bare, perceptive feeling hands wrapped around familiar camera controls.

The list of photographers decreases a lot more when we throw in motion. Not just the motion of the subject being photographed, but the movement of the photographer. So far, we have a situation analogous to travelling at 60 miles an hour in a car, shooting another subject, also in motion.

The list grows shorter still when one adds the z-vector. The third dimension. The vertical plane. This may be akin to photographing a small aircraft from another machine, both travelling at 60 knots, about 2000 feet off the ground. There is movement horizontally and also in a new direction, up and down.

Our once-long list, although still impressive, grows quite shorter when we put the throttle to the firewall. And dial up the velocity, say ten times, to 600 knots. Now, we are sitting in a cold, cramped cockpit with little or no room for movement sideways or forward. In a worst case, only the arms, head and feet are free to move about. The body is firmly pasted onto a hard, not-at-all-designed-for-comfort, chair. The chair has underneath it – for safety, if you can believe that – a rocket capable of hurling a 250-lb pound lump of flesh and bones a hundred or so feet through biting-cold, relatively fast-moving space.

The list takes another great toll when we perturb the situation with more elementary physics. Dial up the G. That is, increase the acceleration due to gravity. In fighter-pilot lingo, pull Gs. How does one explain the sensation? An everyday example is driving a car too fast around a turn. One feels a mild, transverse or sideways force all over the body. The invisible force even pulls at the lightest part of us, our hair. It tugs gently but relentlessly at the skin over our face. Even our lips and eyelids stray imperceptibly to the right or left. This centrifugal force, perhaps, is accelerating us only one and a half Gs. But we do experience the feeling. On a roller coaster, going 60 miles per hour around a banked turn, we may experience up to two or three Gs. That's probably the most a race car driver will pull, three Gs.

At three Gs, all the sensations described above become more perceptible. We now attend to them. We are children all over again, experiencing the unknown, unable to comprehend the invisible hand that pulls and tugs and jerks us about. We seek relief and step on the brakes.

Now let's add just one more nuisance, and do some of the other things diligent professional photographers do while shooting. Think. While dressed in a space suit, sitting on a box of dynamite, inside a cramped can, screaming through space at a fast clip, pulling five or seven or nine Gs . . . think. Think about the images you would like to photograph, think about the background on which you will paint your image. Think about the correct exposure. Think about dramatic lighting. Think about whether there's milk in the refrigerator, or whether you will chuck all over the canopy on the first 720-degree-per-second roll.

Also, the US Navy would like to remind you to think about their $30-million dollar carnival ride. More specifically, please don't break it. Don't push or pull any buttons or toggle switches. Don't turn any dials or knobs. Don't touch the throttle. Don't even think of touching the control stick. And, above all,

RIGHT

A quick change of mount, and 'Wang' is seated in a TA-4J, firing off his Canon at a Skyhawk on the starboard beam. Eliminating camera-shake and reflections from the canopy are only two of the problems encountered in aerial photography

please do not accidentally pull the ejection-seat handle.

And what if there's an in-flight emergency? An engine fire, or worse, a cockpit fire? Think about running through a checklist of detailed options that may save you and your driver. What if your driver wa rendered unconscious and you had to bail out on your own? Think about all the permutations of potential disasters. All the inherent dangers. Or even death. Military fighter pilots do die, dozens each year. And they are well trained. The possibility for disaster permeates the skies. Mother nature and fate know no race, creed, colour, or level of experience. Jet-fighter photography, while 'vogue' on the outside, can be vague and ambiguous and dangerous on the inside.

Cockpit Organization

Normally, I hand-carry all my photo gear in my helmet bag. Three or four cameras with different lenses, one or two extra lenses, 24 new batteries, a four-inch diameter convex mirror, Minolta IV light meter with hemispherical diffuser and five-degree spot-metering attachment, 30 rolls of professional film, (ISO 50-3200), five or more plastic freezer bags with a zippered end, black gaffer's tape, two camera mounting clamps with swivel heads and ball joints, and a pad of blank white paper, ball-point pen, and a fine-tipped indelible marker. The photo gear inside my helmet bag weighs more than four gallons of pasteurized whole milk – 35 lbs – all in one little grocery bag.

After I strap myself into the aircraft, either the driver or plane captain double-checks my straps, belt and hose connections. I then position my gear, putting the cameras to my left and right, just behind my thighs on either side console. I then tape the film bag, which I've reinforced all over with gaffer's tape, to the right side, just underneath the canopy rail, or on the console in front of me. The film bag houses both unexposed and freshly exposed film. I tape the top halfway shut to prevent film from falling out under negative Gs. Anything less than one G, especially approaching zero G, will make most objects, including 185 lbs of jet-fighter photographer, float mercilessly.

Any objects that aren't where they should be are considered FOD, Foreign Object Damage. Pilots don't like FOD. The plane captain detests FOD. The maintenance man absolutely hates FOD. I avoid FOD by keeping all equipment stowed securely either in my helmet bag or the tape-reinforced, zippered plastic bag.

My light meter, on a nylon loop, is around my neck. Hopefully, it won't decapitate me on my way to becoming the fastest man alive, should I eject from the aircraft. The law of statistics suggests that it won't, so I take this calculated risk.

After the pilot and I have gone through our post-start cockpit checks, the plane captain gives the driver a snappy salute. He then smiles and waves at me, wishing me a good hop. The plane captain's gesture always makes me feel more confident. He's done his job well. Now it's up to me to shoot something that will knock his/her socks off, make them even more proud of their hard work and diligent efforts.

The full effort continues as we taxy out to the Hold Short area. More eager, fast-moving young sailors marshall our jet, while they meticulously check for fuel and other fluid leaks, broken or damaged wing or fuselage surfaces, damaged tyres or landing gear assemblages, etc. After their blessing, and the control tower's permission, we taxy onto the runway and position ourselves pointing west. All the while, I am double- and triple-checking my photo gear, cockpit checklists, position of ejection seat handle, oxygen hose and G-suit hose continuity, and a host of other checks that will ensure a safer and more enjoyable flight.

'I'm running 'em up', calls Lt Jim 'Grits' Grimson, my driver, and the

engines roar. With the wheel brakes on, holding back thousands of pounds of thrust from two afterburning engines. 'Wang, we're off!' calls 'Grits'. I wonder if we are at a soap-box derby. His little-boy enthusiasm ignites mine, dumping adrenaline into my bloodstream. I'm on fire! My skin grows goosebumps. The hair on my body stands erect. At attention. I am euphoric. Drunk on absolute, high-voltage energy.

'Grits' releases the bridles on more than a thousand horses, and we rocket down the Miramar raceway. One hundred, one-twenty, one-forty, one hundred and fifty knots. We lift free of the runway at one-fifty, and draw in the landing gear. Now we are slipping through dense, San Diego air at 300-plus knots. I fire off several exposures at the lizard-green and white F-16, joining us off to our right. The camouflaged jet against a lush, green Torrey Pines golf course is incredible. That's why they call it camouflage.

General Jet-Fighter Photography

As we head west to Papa-five, one of TOPGUN's working areas off the coast of southern California, I check that each camera is loaded with fresh film and batteries, and that the light meter has a fresh battery, too. I then relax a bit and enjoy the ride en route to Papa-five

Since we have already briefed the mission, I'm not too concerned about the weather, position of the sun, cloud cover, or potential backgrounds. I have in mind the various set ups we will perform and shoot, so it's simply a matter of the pilot's telling me we are ready, and my calling, 'Fight's on!'

Intuitively, I always know where the sun is, regardless of whether we have dialed up six or eight Gs in a twenty-degree-per second turn. The reflection of the sun off our canopy, sometimes causing a glare, can make or break a shot. Careful preplanning obviates worry about unwanted reflections.

When shooting directly into the sun, I take an exposure reading off various parts of our own aircraft, exposed to different levels of sunlight. Otherwise, I take reflected-light measurements off the target jet, using the camera's internal exposure meter. Framing the target jet is usually a challenge, regardless of pre-flight preparation. This situation is true, especially if I want to show motion. Showing motion in a still picture requires skill, to say the least. Under ordinary, one-G conditions, like those on earth, one can simply pan the camera, following a moving subject, and point and shoot. For me, though, the equation complicates itself above six Gs, literally forcing me to deal not only with correct exposure and framing and composition, but also holding some 70 lbs of camera that the laws of physics, against my wants, eases into my lap.

Although a lot of practice doesn't necessarily ensure perfection, or even success, in this aerial game – especially under high Gs, when my socks are rolling down in perfect little donuts about my ankles– . lots of practice alleviates my possibly shooting off 20 exposures of my scuffed black flight boots.

Photographing from high-performance jets is a challenge unto itself. Some

RIGHT

Controlling its position by use of airbrakes, one of TOPGUN's TF-16Ns formates off the starboard quarter of the TA-4J 'camera-ship', which is probably a lot closer than this wide-angle shot suggests. The F-16N is basically an F-16C with the 28,982-1b (13,600 kg) F110-GE-100 engine, a stronger wing, ALR-69 radar warning receiver, ALE-40 chaff/flare dispensers, Air Combat Manoeuvring Instrumentation (ACMI) capability, and a unique camouflage scheme. The gun and ASPJ provisions are deleted, and the Westinghouse APG-68 radar is replaced by the lighter APG-66 from the F-16A

jets are easier and more comfortable to ride in. The TA-4 trainer is, by far, the most uncomfortable and demanding. It's like donning ten tons of chainmail that was designed and built for some guy two sizes smaller than me. When Mr Edward Heinemann designed the venerable fighter, he had in mind a fleet of very little fighter pilots, dolls it seems like. One seemingly must grease his body with petroleum jelly, then slide into a sardine can, sans one's piscine neighbours. Once pinned down in the cockpit, movement is severly limited. For example, it's very difficult to photograph comfortably more than 45 degrees behind me. Turning backward is impossible, unless I unstrap all that hardware keeping me happily secured in the hot seat. And the canopy, bearing scratches older than most college-aged kids, often impedes vision. I usually reach far forward, up or down, to peek through a fairly clear section of canopy. The TA-4 Skyhawk, while an absolute riot to fly in, is not the finest photographic platform.

In sharp contrast, the F-14 Tomcat is the 'Cadillac' of jet fighters, offering a comfortable spacious cockpit with unlimited field of view. The best feature for me, aside from the roominess, is the jet-like airconditioner, blowing Arctic winds across my perspiration-drenched flight suit. During an average two-hour photo mission, I shed a half-gallon of perspiration, more than four pounds of water and salt. In the least, the Tomcat's airconditioner assuages discomfort from 'diaper rash', and allows me to shoot in relative luxury. Plus, the large surface area of the canopy provides a better medium through which to photograph. The ample side-console area gives me more room to stow gear, especially cameras. And the large handle on top of the front console is excellent for mounting a camera. In the same vein, the F-16N 'Viper' is also well suited as an aerial photo platform. Although it's not as roomy as the 'Turkey' (the pilots' affectionate name for the F-14), its high-tech look and feel give me the distinct impression of comfort and flexibility. The biggest drawback, though, is the bubble canopy, the concavity of which almost always produces glare and/or internal reflection off the canopy, both, at times, producing unwanted side effects. So, it takes very careful planning, especially positioning the sun, to shoot from the 'Viper'.

But, hands down, there's nothing like pulling eight plus Gs in a winged Ferrari. Flying in the 'Viper' – small, racy, very fast, highly manoeuvrable– is almost indescribable. I feel that when I sit in the cockpit and strap in, I'm spray painting on a film of body oil. A warm wetsuit of comfort. And when the afterburner ignites, I more than just accelerate, I move! For me, the feeling of pulling high Gs in such a small environment is orgasmic at worst. A 'Viper' flight is still the hottest ride in town! During my time away from high-tech brain research, there's little I enjoy more than hanging out with fighter pilots and flying in rock-n-roll jets. Regardless of all the potential danger. Life is too short not to 'become the one you dream you can be'. – Goethe

RIGHT
A Tomcat's RIO during a night-time sortie, rendered green by the illumination of his radar display. A remarkable development for its day, the Hughes AWG-9 can track 24 targets simultaneously while engaging six, and continuing to search for further targets. Its outstanding range allows AIM-54 firings to take place at distances of around 100 nm (185 km). In the Vietnam War, three of the five American aces were Phantom II backseaters (one Navy RIO and two USAF WSOs)

The Tomcat RIO goes head-down, the handles of his Martin-Baker ejection seat standing up like ears on his bone-dome

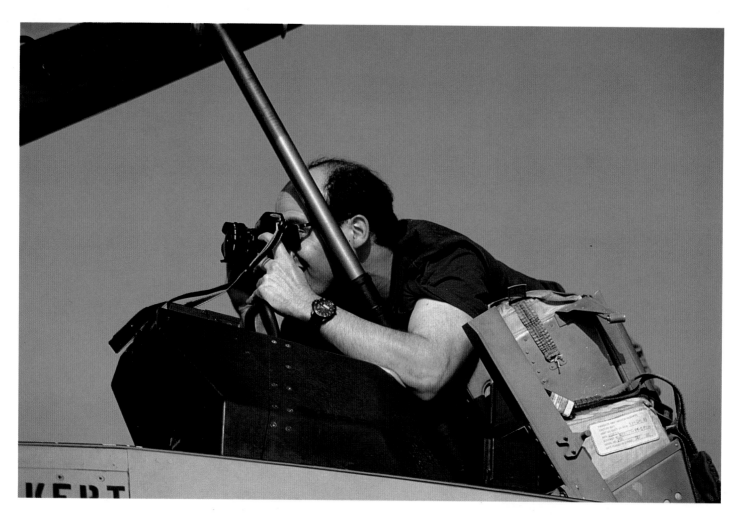

ABOVE

In the hold of a VAW-110 Greyhound, Loadmaster John Coffin briefs Donna Brackeen on the forthcoming photographic sortie. The Grumman C-2A carrier on-board delivery (COD) aircraft is basically a derivative of the E-2 Hawkeye, with a fuselage designed for the carriage of cargo. In this instance its most important feature is its rear loading ramp, which (like that of the C-130) facilitates head-on photographs of aircraft

ABOVE LEFT

Leaning on the glare-shield, 'Wang' assesses the rear view from the cockpit of a TOPGUN TF-16N. This photograph illustrates the low sill-height of the F-16 cockpit, and the unusually large inclination of the ejection seats (Photo by Ensign Jon 'Lloyd' Nolan)

LEFT

Garner ascends to the rear seat of TA-4J Skyhawk '57' for another photographic sortie. The heavy framework and multiplicity of rear-view mirrors are noteworthy design features (Photo by Ensign Jon 'Lloyd' Nolan)

ABOVE
Photographs taken, inflight plane captain Jeffrey Pate of VAW-110 and Dean Garner enjoy the sunset from the rear loading ramp of the C-2A (Photo by Donna Brackeen)

ABOVE RIGHT
Greyhound meets Skyhawk. Suitably restrained against extra-vehicular activity, Jeffrey Pate of VAW-110 watches Dean Garner photograph A-4F '53' flown by Lt Dave 'Shooter' Vanderschoot (Photo by Donna Brackeen)

RIGHT
Greyhound meets Hawkeye. Inflight plane captain Jeffrey Pate watches 'Wang' photograph an E-2C, which, like the C-2A, hails from VAW-110, the Pacific coast training unit for both aircraft types (Photo by Donna Brackeen)

ABOVE

Dean Garner signals to Lt Vanderschoot in the A-4F that he should make a right turn, as they fly over the southern California coastline (Photo by Donna Brackeen)

RIGHT

Rear view from the TF-16N, with an A-4 flying off the starboard wingtip, as an F-16N makes a firing pass

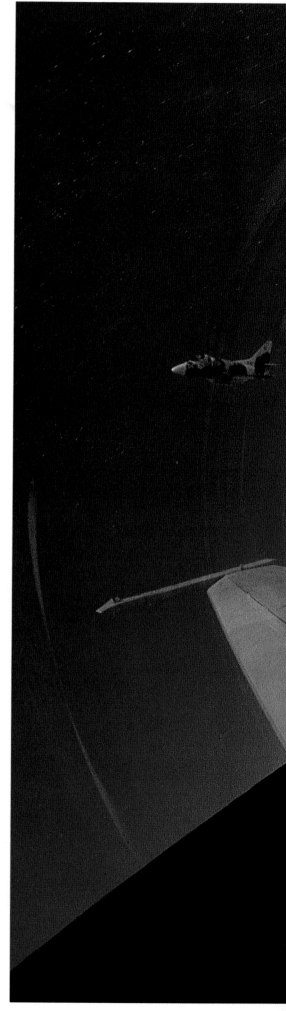

The author experiences considerable positive G the TF-16N makes a turn off the coast near NAS Miramar